Van Wolverton's Guide to
DOS 6

VAN WOLVERTON
ONE OF THE WORLD'S LEADING EXPERTS

RANDOM HOUSE
ELECTRONIC PUBLISHING

New York

Van Wolverton's Guide to DOS 6

Copyright © 1993 by Van Wolverton

Published in the United States by Random House, Inc., New York, and simultaneously in Canada by Random House of Canada, Limited.

Manufactured in the United States of America.

Revised Edition

ISBN 0-679-74469-X

New York   Toronto   London   Sydney   Auckland

CONTENTS

INTRODUCTION

Yet another book about DOS. How can there be so many books on one program? What's so different about this book?

Well, maybe it's easier to describe what this book *isn't*: It isn't very big, for starters; it fits beside your computer quite nicely; it won't tip over your nightstand; and it doesn't loom on the horizon like some digitally-enhanced *War and Peace*. There's no disk of programs to enhance DOS, no wall chart that summarizes every known DOS command and function, no cents-off coupons you can use to buy your favorite software.

What you're holding is a brief introduction to DOS, the program required to operate any IBM PC-compatible computer. (DOS stands for *Disk Operating System*, a program stored on Disks that Operates a computer System). DOS must be running on a computer before you can run any other program, so at some point after you start using your computer, you're going to encounter DOS.

The emphasis of this book is on the DOS Shell, the part of DOS that displays menus of commands and lists of files and lets you use a mouse—or the keyboard, if you prefer—to choose commands and files from those menus and lists. The alternative to the Shell is to use DOS commands; the book also covers the most common commands you'll need.

It's Not a Textbook

This guide is meant to be used at the computer, not read and studied like a textbook. Each chapter consists of a series of related examples that show you how to use DOS to manage your programs, files, and disks. When you complete the examples in the twelve chapters, you'll have a good grounding in the fundamentals of DOS and its most frequently used commands.

You won't find a complete reference to the DOS commands here. You've already got one of those: The *MS-DOS User's Guide and Reference* that came with the program. That manual is the official, authoritative word on every aspect of DOS. It may not be the clearest document around, but it's nothing if not thorough. After you finish the examples in this smaller, less authoritative book that you're holding now, you'll find that it's much easier to understand what the MS-DOS manual tells you.

Parts 1 and 2: The Shell and DOS Commands

This book is divided into two parts. The first part, Chapters 1 through 7, covers the Shell. Because the Shell packages the commands in a visual structure and lets you pick and choose what you want to do with a minimum of memorization, the Shell is the simplest way to get started using DOS. Although it doesn't include all the capabilities of DOS, the Shell handles most of the the routine functions. If you just use your computer to run a few programs and never add any hardware or software, you might never need to leave the friendly confines of the Shell.

But sooner or later you'll probably have to operate DOS from the command prompt. Part II, chapters 8 through 13, covers the most common DOS commands, showing you through examples how to manage your files and disks and even how to do a bit of customizing so that DOS more closely matches how you use your computer.

The best way—in fact, the only productive way—to use this book is to sit down at your computer with this guide beside you, start with chapter 1, and go through the examples from beginning to end. You won't need any other programs or books; the examples use only programs and files that come with DOS or that you can create yourself. Depending on how long you want to spend at a time, you should be able to complete the entire book in two or three evenings. Bon voyage.

—Van Wolverton
Rubicon
Alberton, Montana
February 1993

PART I

THE DOS SHELL

CHAPTER

1

A QUICK TOUR OF THE
DOS SHELL

A home base is a familiar place to return to after venturing out into the world. You can arrange the furniture the way you want it, stock the shelves with food you like, install the tools and toys you need (or want).

Think of the DOS Shell as your home base for your ventures into the computer world. It will soon become a familiar place that reflects your needs and desires. Just as you decorate your house and rear-range the furniture to make it comfortable and functional, you'll arrange the files, programs, and commands displayed by the Shell to suit the way you use your computer.

Although this first tour of the Shell is a quick one, it covers quite a bit of ground and serves two equally important purposes: It shows you how to operate the Shell and guides you through some examples that make sure the Shell on your system matches the illustrations in the book.

If you're ready to start the tour, turn on your computer. As it comes to life, your computer flexes its muscles a little, sending out messages to confirm that the memory, keyboard, drives, and other components are all right. As it does this, it may display some infor-mation on the screen. When this start-up process is done, the last line of text on your screen should be the letter C followed by some punctuation and a blinking line:

```
C:\_
```

This is called the *DOS prompt.* Depending on how your system is set up, you may see more or less following the capital C than what is shown above. That's not important now; what is important is the letter C, which is how DOS refers to your computer's hard disk drive. (DOS refers to floppy disk drives as A and B).

The blinking underline is the *cursor,* which draws your attention to the spot on the screen where anything you type will appear. You tell DOS what to do by typing a command at the DOS prompt, which is why this line on the screen that begins with the DOS prompt and ends with the cursor is often called the *command line.*

You can type many different commands at the DOS prompt— you'll use some of them later in this book—but the only command you'll need for a while is the one that tells DOS to start the Shell. To issue this command, type the following (press Enter when you have typed it):

```
dosshell
```

As the Shell starts, it takes a few moments to check each file on your hard disk. When it has finished loading, the image you see on your screen should look quite a bit like this:

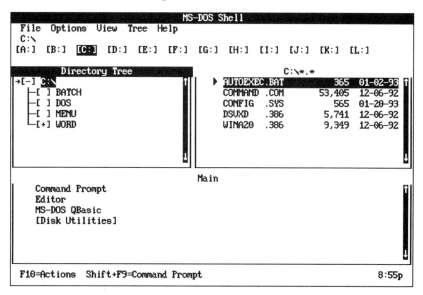

This Shell screen shows you some of the directories and files on your hard disk, along with some commands and other organizational features. Your screen won't look exactly like this because you have a different collection of directories and files and probably fewer disk drives. Also, the DOS Shell starts up looking the same as it did the last time it was used, so if you or someone else has run the DOS Shell on your computer and changed any of the settings, it may not look the same as this. But that's OK, because one of the first things you're going to do is make your screen look like the illustration. (Even if your screen looks just like the illustration, go through the following examples anyway. You'll get some valuable practice.)

You'll use the keyboard during the first part of this tour. A bit later, you'll start using the mouse.

Using the Keyboard to Tour the Menus

You control the Shell with instructions called *commands*. Rather than having to memorize commands and type them, you choose the command you want from one of several lists of related commands, called *menus*. The Shell displays the names of the menus at the top of the screen. Depending on what you're doing, the names of the menus can change; right now the Shell should be displaying the names of five menus: File, Options, View, Tree, and Help:

```
                          MS-DOS Shell
 File  Options  View  Tree  Help
```

To choose a command, you must first choose the menu that contains it. To choose a menu, press and release the Alt key. The Shell highlights the word *File* in the top row. Once you have highlighted the name of the File menu, you can highlight a different menu name by pressing the right or left arrow key. Press the right arrow key once, and the Shell highlights the name of the next menu, *Options*. Press the left arrow key, and *File* is highlighted again.

To display the commands in the File menu, press Enter. You should see the commands in the File menu:

```
 File

 Open
 Run...
 Print
 Associate...
 Search...
 View File Contents    F9

 Move...               F7
 Copy...               F8
 Delete...            Del
 Rename...
 Change Attributes...

 Create Directory...

 Select All
 Deselect All

 Exit             Alt+F4
```

When you have displayed the commands in a menu, you can use the arrow keys to display the commands in an adjoining menu, just as you used the arrow keys to highlight the names of different menus. For example, press the right arrow key, and the Shell displays the commands in the Options menu:

```
 Options 
┌──────────────────────────────────┐
│ Confirmation...                  │
│ File Display Options...          │
│ Select Across Directories        │
│ Show Information...               │
│ Enable Task Swapper               │
│ Display...                        │
│ Colors...                         │
└──────────────────────────────────┘
```

Restoring the Shell's Original State

To make sure that the examples in the book work properly and your screen looks the same as the illustrations, the next few examples have you check some of the Shell settings. Don't worry about understanding or remembering these steps; the only purpose is to restore the original state of the Shell and give you some practice choosing menus and commands.

Right now, the first command in the Options menu (*Confirmation*) should be highlighted. Press Enter to choose the Confirmation command. The Shell has to get some information from you in order to carry out this command, so it displays a questionnaire titled *Confirmation*:

```
       ┌─ Confirmation ──────────────────┐
       │                                 │
       │  [X] Confirm on Delete          │
       │  [X] Confirm on Replace         │
       │  [X] Confirm on Mouse Operation │
       │                                 │
       │                                 │
       │  ( OK )   ( Cancel )   ( Help ) │
       └─────────────────────────────────┘
```

There should be an X enclosed in brackets—*[X]*—before each of the three options, as shown in the illustration. If one of the options isn't preceded by an X, press the Tab key until the underscore is in front of that option and press the space bar to select that option; an X should appear between the brackets. If all the options are preceded by an X (or after you have made sure they do), press Enter to complete the Confirmation command.

You're going to check a few more things with the Options menu. Press Alt again to highlight the name of the File menu. This time, however, don't press the right arrow key to highlight the name of the Options menu. Notice that the first letter of each menu name is displayed in a different color (or shade of gray). You can tell the Shell to display the commands in any menu by pressing the first letter of its name after you press and release Alt (you don't have to press Enter).

Press O, and the Shell displays the Options menu again. Notice that here, too, one letter in each command—usually the first letter—is displayed in a different color, just like the first letter of each menu name was displayed in a different color. The meaning is the same: You can choose any command by pressing this highlighted letter without pressing Enter. Press D to choose the Display command. The Shell displays another questionnaire titled *Screen Display Mode* (these questionnaires are called *dialog boxes*):

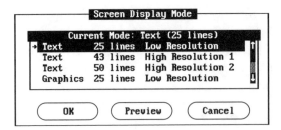

Canceling a Dialog Box

When you're using the Shell, sometimes you'll choose a command that displays a dialog box, then decide that you don't want to continue. To cancel a dialog box, all you need do is press Esc. Press Esc now; the dialog box goes away, and the Shell is back the way it was before you chose the Display command.

But you do want to check some settings in the Screen Display Mode dialog box, so press Alt+O, then D again. Your selection in this dialog box determines whether the Shell displays just text characters or both text and graphics, and how many rows can be displayed. For now, the top line inside the box should read *Current Mode: Text (25 lines)*. If it doesn't, press the up arrow key until the first line (*Text 25 lines Low Resolution*) is highlighted, then press Enter. If it does, press Esc to remove the dialog box.

Next, you'll check the settings in the dialog box displayed when you choose *File Display Options* from the Options menu. Press Alt+O to display the Options menu, then press F; the Shell displays a dialog box titled *File Display Options*:

The settings in this dialog box should be just as shown. The information after the *Name* label is highlighted, meaning that any text you type right now will replace it; if the highlighted text is not *.* (that's an asterisk, a period, and another asterisk), type *.* now (but don't press Enter yet).

The *Display hidden/system files* and *Descending order* options should not be preceded by an X in brackets; if either is, press Tab to move the underscore to that option and then press the space bar to remove the X. If *Name* isn't preceded by a dot in parentheses— (•)—in the list of options under *Sort by*, press Tab to move the underscore to the option that does have the dot, then press the up arrow key until the dot moves to *Name*. When everything agrees with the illustration, press Enter.

Using the Mouse to Choose Commands from the Menu

Up to this point, your mouse has been sitting neglected beside your keyboard. It's time to put it to use. If you've never used a mouse before, it will feel unfamiliar at first, but take heart: Like riding a bicycle, mousing around the screen quickly becomes second nature —it's even easier to learn, and you can't tip over.

As you slide the mouse around, you should see a small square moving around the screen. This is the *mouse pointer* (or, more commonly, the pointer). To choose a menu with the mouse, you move the mouse until the pointer is over the menu name, then press and release the left button; this action is called *clicking*.

Display the Options menu again, this time by clicking it with your mouse (if you don't have a mouse, press Alt+O). Neither the *Select Across Directories* nor *Enable Task Swapper* command should have a dot in front of it, as shown in the following illustration:

```
 Options 
┌──────────────────────────────┐
│ Confirmation...              │
│ File Display Options...      │
│ Select Across Directories    │
│ Show Information...           │
│ Enable Task Swapper           │
│ Display...                    │
│ Colors...                     │
└──────────────────────────────┘
```

If either one is preceded by a dot, click on the command name (this is how you choose a command with the mouse). Now display the Options menu again; the dot should have disappeared. If both commands were preceded by a dot, repeat the process to eliminate the other dot.

Combining Steps

You can combine choosing a menu and choosing a command into a single mouse action by holding the left mouse button down after displaying the menu, then moving the mouse so the pointer moves down the menu (moving the mouse while holding down the button is called *dragging*). As the pointer moves down the menu, the commands it passes over are highlighted. Releasing the mouse button while a command is highlighted chooses that command.

If you're dragging the pointer down the list of commands displayed in a menu and decide that you don't want to choose a command from that menu after all, simply drag the mouse pointer out of the menu and release the button.

There's one more thing to check. Display the View menu (click on the menu name or press Alt+V). The Shell displays the View commands:

```
┌─────┐
│View │
├─────┴──────────────────────────┐
│ Single File List               │
│ Dual File Lists                │
│ All Files                      │
│ Program/File Lists             │
│ Program List                   │
│                                │
│ Repaint Screen  Shift+F5       │
│ Refresh         F5             │
└────────────────────────────────┘
```

The commands on this menu control what the Shell displays. The *Program/File Lists* command on your menu should be dimmer than the other commands, as shown in the illustration. If it isn't dimmer, choose *Program/File Lists* (click on the command or press F).

If your screen didn't look much like the first illustration in this chapter before, it should now. Now that you've gone to all that work to restore the original state of the Shell, you'll change it.

Customizing Your Display

The quality of displays has improved dramatically in the past few years. The Shell works with monochrome or color displays that can show only text or both text and graphics and offers several degrees of resolution for each. When the Shell is installed, however, it assumes the minimum display capability. You can customize the Shell to take advantage of the type of monitor you have and to suit your taste in color.

One of the settings you checked (or changed) a few moments ago told the Shell to display text only in low resolution—the lowest-common denominator setting, available on all computers. It's time to look at some of the other display options.

You may have noticed earlier that some commands are followed by an ellipsis (three dots). This tells you that the Shell will prompt you to provide some additional information before it carries out the command. Display the Options menu again (click *Options* or press Alt+O):

```
 Options

 Confirmation...
 File Display Options...
 Select Across Directories
 Show Information...
 Enable Task Swapper
 Display...
 Colors...
```

Nearly every command on this menu, including the Display command that controls the screen display, is followed by an ellipsis. Choose *Display* (click *Display* or press D). The Shell displays the Screen Display Mode dialog box:

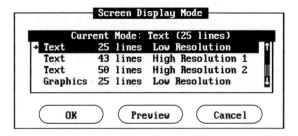

```
                Screen Display Mode

           Current Mode: Text (25 lines)
 →  Text       25 lines  Low Resolution      ↑
    Text       43 lines  High Resolution 1
    Text       50 lines  High Resolution 2
    Graphics   25 lines  Low Resolution      ↓


    (    OK    )    (   Preview   )    (  Cancel  )
```

This dialog box lists the display modes your display can use. The top line inside the box should read *Current Mode: Text (25 lines)*, and the first item in the list—*Text 25 lines Low Resolution*—should be highlighted. To match the illustrations in the rest of the book, you're going to change to medium-resolution graphics.

The dialog box can show only four display modes at one time. If your display supports more than four modes, the additional modes are out of sight above or below the list. You scroll up or down the list by pressing the arrow keys or clicking the mouse on the up and down arrows at the right side of the list. If you don't have a mouse, press the down arrow key to highlight *Graphics 34 lines Medium Resolution 2*, and press Enter. If you're using a mouse, click on the down arrow until *Graphics 34 lines Medium Resolution 2* is visible.

Double-Clicking, Another Shortcut

Now that you can see the choice you want, you could choose it by clicking it, then clicking *OK* at the bottom of the dialog box. You can eliminate a step by clicking the choice twice in rapid succession; in effect, the first click highlights your choice and the second click confirms it, just as clicking on *OK* would. This is called *double-clicking*; you'll find that you can often use it to choose items from a list and avoid a second step to confirm your choice.

Double-click *Graphics 34 lines Medium Resolution 2*. The Shell screen goes dark for a moment, then returns, but now it looks somewhat different:

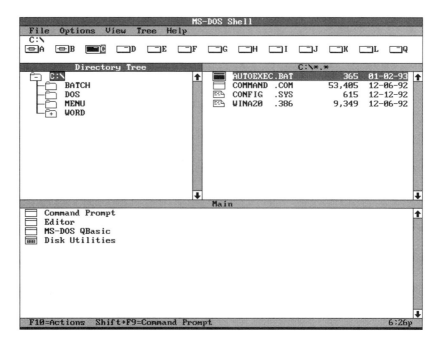

Many of the elements on the screen are now represented by small pictures. These pictures, often called *icons*, are designed to give a hint as to what they represent or what you can do with them. These icons tend to make the information on the screen easier to understand, but they don't change the meaning of anything. So even with this different display, you move around the Shell and choose commands the same way.

Pick a Color

Depending on the type of display you have, the Shell can use either two or four shades of gray, or up to 16 colors. The Shell comes with eight predefined color schemes with names like Basic Blue and Hot Pink; to see which one you're using and try out a new one, choose *Colors* from the Options menu (press Alt+O, then O, or click on *Options* and *Colors*). The Shell displays the Color Scheme dialog box:

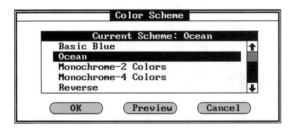

This dialog box is almost identical to the Screen Display Mode dialog box, but it lists color schemes instead of display modes. The top line inside the box identifies the current color scheme, and the entry for that scheme is highlighted in the list.

Asking for Help

The Shell doesn't leave you on your own while you're using it; descriptions of Shell features and instructions for using them are stored on your disk and available with the stroke of a key. To see what help the Shell offers on this dialog box, press F1, the help key. The Shell displays a box titled *MS-DOS Shell Help* and subtitled *Color Scheme Option*:

The text describes the dialog box you were looking at; notice that at the end is an entry in a different color that reads *Changing Colors*. It's in a different color to tell you that the Shell will display additional information if you choose it; the entry should be highlighted, so either press Enter or double-click it. The Shell changes the subtitle of the MS-DOS Shell Help box to *Changing Colors*:

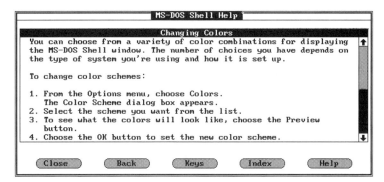

These are detailed instructions for using the Color Scheme dialog box. The information is longer than the window, so you'll have to scroll to read all of it. When you have read the information, either press Esc or click on *Close* to get rid of the help information and return to the Color Scheme dialog box.

Back to screen colors. To use the keyboard to choose a new color scheme, you use the up and down arrow keys to scroll through the choices, then press Enter when the one you want is highlighted. To use the mouse, you click the up or down arrows at the right side of the list to scroll through the choices, then double-click the one you want.

Try some different color schemes to see what they look like (if you're using a monochrome display, you'll have to limit your choices to *Monochrome-2 Colors, Monochrome-4 Colors,* and *Reverse*). Pick the one you like best; the Shell will use it thereafter—when you quit the Shell and restart it, or even turn your computer off and turn it back on.

In addition to pressing F1, you can also use the Help menu to get information about the Shell. Display the Help menu:

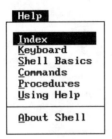

Each of the choices in the Help menu displays a list of several related topics you can choose. To see how it works, choose *Using Help*; the Shell displays the MS-DOS Shell Help window, subtitled *Using Help*:

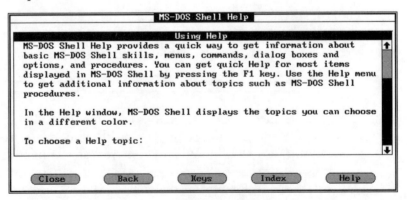

Again, there's too much text to fit on the screen, so you'll have to scroll to read it all. At the end of the text is the list of further topics, each in a different color to tell you that you can choose them. The first item, *Requesting Help Directly,* is highlighted; press Enter to choose it. The Shell displays its help box:

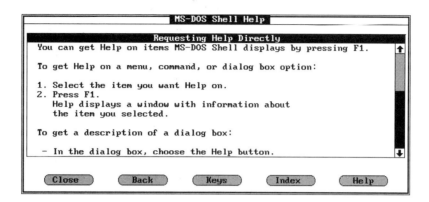

Here are detailed instructions for displaying help information al-most anywhere in the Shell. After you have become somewhat famil-iar with the layout and operation of the Shell, the online help may be all the additional information you need.

Press Esc to clear the help boxes from the screen.

Chapter Review

This chapter covered a lot of ground pretty quickly. Don't be too concerned if everything you have seen isn't completely clear; you'll have plenty of practice to reinforce these techniques in the next few chapters. The most important points covered in this chapter:

- Type `dosshell` at the DOS prompt to start the Shell.

- To choose a command with the keyboard, press Alt plus the first letter of a menu to display the commands in the menu, then either press the down arrow key to highlight the com-mand and press Enter, or type the highlighted letter in the command name.

- To choose a command with the mouse, click on the name of the menu, then either hold down the mouse button and drag the pointer until the command is highlighted and release the mouse button, or release the mouse button and click on the command.

- To choose an item from a list with the keyboard, highlight the item with the up or down arrow key, then press Enter.

- To choose an item from a list with the mouse, either click on the item and then click on OK, or double-click (click twice in rapid succession) the item.

- Use the Tab key to move to different items in a dialog box.

- Press Esc to cancel a dialog box or a menu.

- Press F1 or use the Help menu to get online information about the Shell.

CHAPTER

2

WORKING WITH DIRECTORIES

19

Just as a paper file contains documents that you have saved, a computer file contains information you have saved. Just as you label your file folders so you can find them later, every computer file has its own name. Most of the work you do with your computer, in fact, involves files. You use various application programs, such as word processors and drawing programs, to create or change files that are stored on your disk. Later, you might print these files, copy them to a floppy disk, or even delete them when they are no longer needed.

But unless you have just a few paper files, you need some sort of organized system to store the files. If you just threw them all in a box, it would take longer and longer to find the one you wanted as your collection grew, even though each one was carefully labeled. Similarly, you need some sort of organized system to store your computer files. This chapter shows you how to set up such a system on your disk.

If you're continuing from Chapter 1 or if you just turned your system on, your screen should look much like the following illustration:

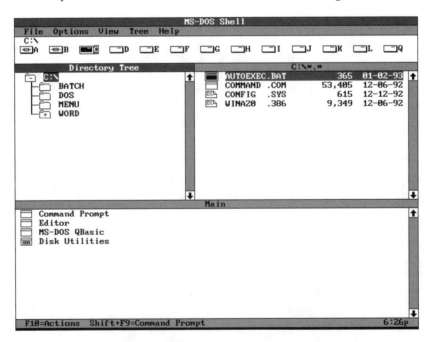

The number and names of the directories and files will be different, but the general layout of the screen should be the same. If your screen doesn't look like this, choose *Program/File Lists* from the View menu (click on *View* and *Program/File Lists*, or press Alt+V and F).

The File List Area

In Chapter 1, you used the keyboard and mouse to choose commands that controlled what the Shell displayed and the colors used on the screen. Now it's time to look at the Shell screen in more detail. You've already worked with the list of menu names; the screen you're looking at now is made up of three major areas:

- Below the menu names, the series of small drawings, each followed by a letter, represent the disk drives attached to your computer. The letter is the name DOS gives to each drive; the drive you're using now is highlighted.

- The top half of the main portion of the screen is divided into two lists. The left side, titled *Directory Tree*, shows the names of your directories; the directory you're using now is highlighted (the first directory in the list, *C:*, should be highlighted). The right side lists the name, size, and date of last change of each file in the highlighted directory; its title includes the name of the highlighted directory (right now it should read *C:*.**). This area, called the *file list*, is described in this chapter.

- The bottom part of the screen, titled *Main*, lists the names of the programs you can run. This area, called the *program list*, is described in Chapter 4.

To work in any of these areas, you either press Tab until the title of the area is highlighted or click anywhere in the area. For example, press the Tab key a few times (or click in different areas of the screen) and see how different titles are highlighted. Stop with the title of the upper left area (*Directory Tree*) highlighted.

You'll spend most of your time in the Shell using the file list to move, copy, delete, and otherwise manage your files. So that you can see as many directories and files as possible while you're working with the file list, choose *Single File List* from the View menu. This removes the program list from the bottom of the screen, allowing the directory tree and file list to take up the full screen:

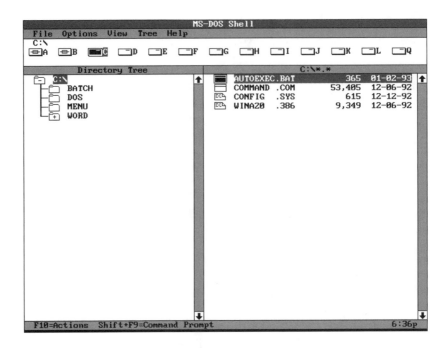

If the title line on the left side of the screen that reads *Directory Tree* isn't highlighted, press the Tab key until it is highlighted (or click anywhere in the left side of the screen). If the first line under the title line (*C:*) isn't highlighted, press the Home key (or click on that line).

Directories to Hold Your Files

If there were room for only a few files on a disk, locating any specific file would be easy: You'd look at the list of file names and choose the one you wanted. That's pretty much how things were in the early days of personal computers, but hard disk capacity has soared. Now it's possible to store thousands of files on a hard disk. And because nature, real estate developers, and computer users all seem to have the same dislike for empty space, most hard disks fill rapidly.

If you tossed all your paper files in one drawer, you'd soon have a problem finding the file you need; to make the files easier to find, you organize them in some manner. You might, for example, put all your bills into one folder, your correspondence in another, and bank statements in another. DOS lets you create a similar filing system for your hard disk, made up of *directories* that hold your files.

For all practical purposes, you can create as many directories on your hard disk as you need to organize your files to suit the way you use your computer. You'll probably store each program you use in its own directory, and you might create separate directories for different sorts of projects or documents, such as budgets, letters, and tax records.

Every disk starts with one directory. Not only can you can store files in this directory, you can create other directories in it. These additional directories—often called *subdirectories*—can also hold both files and yet more subdirectories. This is much like the process you would use to store paper files in a filing cabinet. If you think of your hard disk as a filing cabinet, each of the drawers represents a directory, each of the large green dividers is a subdirectory, and the individual file folders are files.

The Root Directory

Like a file, each directory has its own name so you can find the one you want. A picture of the directories on your hard disk, with that first directory branching into subdirectories that might branch further into still more subdirectories, might remind you of a tree. For this reason, that first directory is usually called the *root directory* of the disk.

Although you name all the additional directories that you create, you can't name the root directory; DOS—and the Shell—use a shorthand notation for its name: the backslash symbol (\). That's why the highlighted name at the top of the left side of your screen reads *C:*—the C: is the name of your hard disk, and the \ means the root directory.

When DOS was installed on your hard disk, it created a directory named DOS and placed most of its files in it. If other programs are installed on your hard disk, they, too, are probably stored in their own directories. Just as no two houses look exactly alike because their owners have different furnishings, no two disks contain exactly the same directories and files because their owners use their computers in different ways.

The Directory Tree

The left side of your screen is titled *Directory Tree* because it shows you both the names of your directories and how they are structured. Right now it should look like this:

The list of files on the right side of the screen shows the name, size, and date of last change of each file in the directory highlighted on the left side of the screen. The root directory is highlighted, so you're looking at a description of the files in the root directory on your hard disk.

Because no two disks contain exactly the same directories and files, the file and directory names on your screen don't exactly match the illustration. The general layout, however, should be the same, and some files in the illustration may also appear on your screen (for example, AUTOEXEC.BAT).

If you highlight a different directory, the list of files changes. Press the down arrow key to highlight the directory named DOS. Now the title bar on the right side starts out *C:\DOS*, and the list of files should look something like this:

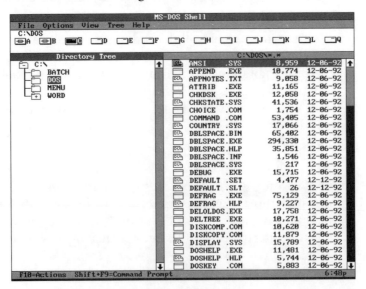

These files contain the programs and data that DOS needs. If your screen doesn't look exactly like the preceding illustration, carry on; everything is fine. As DOS evolves, the names, sizes, and dates of its files may change, but the fundamental operation remains the same.

Scrolling through a List

To see just how many files DOS uses, press the Tab key to highlight the title bar on the right side of the screen—this tells you that now you're working in the list of files—and hold down the down arrow key to scroll through the list (to use the mouse, click on the down arrow at the lower right of the file list). This is the same technique you used in the first chapter to scroll through the list of screen display mode options.

While the list is scrolling, notice the bar that moves down the right side of the file list toward the down arrow. The narrow column down which the bar moves is called the *scroll bar*; if you think of the top of this column as the beginning of the list and the bottom of the column as the end, the moving bar (the *scroll marker*) shows you where the displayed portion is located in the entire list. Continue scrolling until the scroll marker is at the bottom of the scroll bar.

Using the mouse, you can also scroll through a list by dragging the scroll marker up and down. Try it. Move the mouse pointer to the scroll marker, press and hold the left mouse button, and move the scroll marker up a bit; the list of files scrolls back up. Release the mouse button.

Using the keyboard, you can move quickly through a list using the PgUp, PgDn, Home, and End keys. Click once in the file list area. Press the Home key; the beginning of the list is displayed and the first file is highlighted (the position of the scroll marker confirms that it's the beginning of the list). Now press the End key; the end of the list is displayed and the last file is highlighted. The PgUp and PgDn keys move through the list one screenful at a time toward the beginning or end of the list.

You can use these techniques to scroll through any list that the Shell displays.

Creating a New Directory

So that you can experiment more with directories and files without the risk of losing some valuable data, you'll create some new directories. You've got to move back to the directory tree, so press Shift+ Tab (hold down either shift key and press the Tab key). You've moved from one area of the Shell screen to the next by pressing Tab; pressing Shift+Tab does the same, but in the reverse direction.

Creating a new directory is easy: the only tricky part is making sure that you highlight the directory that is to contain the new directory before you choose the Create Directory command. In the following examples, you're going to create a few directories that you'll use in the next examples.

Suppose that part of your job is to prepare the budget for several departments; in addition to the budgets, you also prepare a written report and some charts, and you save the old charts. Just as you might write some labels on file folders to hold these documents, you'll create four directories to hold the files:

- A directory named BUDGETS in the root directory
- Two directories named REPORTS and CHARTS in the new directory BUDGETS
- A directory named OLD in the directory named CHARTS

First you'll create a new directory named BUDGETS in the root directory. Start by pressing Home to highlight the root directory (C:\), then choose *Create Directory* from the File menu. The Shell displays the Create Directory dialog box:

The Shell is waiting for you to type the name of the new directory. Type budgets and press Enter.

When the dialog box disappears, the directory tree should show your new directory BUDGETS on the branch that comes out of the bottom of the root directory. Highlight BUDGETS and check the file list; it says *No files in selected directory*. Of course there aren't, you just created this directory. It's empty.

You need two subdirectories in BUDGETS. Follow these steps to create two directories named REPORTS and CHARTS:

1. Move the highlight down to BUDGETS, which is to contain the new directories.
2. Choose *Create Directory* from the File menu.
3. Type reports and press Enter.
4. Choose *Create Directory* from the File menu.
5. Type charts and press Enter.

Finally, follow these steps to create a subdirectory named OLD in CHARTS:

1. Highlight CHARTS.
2. Choose *Create Directory* from the File menu.
3. Type old and press Enter.

Your directory tree should now include a branch that looks like this:

Notice that the Shell displays the directories in alphabetic order—CHARTS appears before REPORTS, even though you created REPORTS first.

The Path to a Directory

Press the up arrow key to highlight BUDGETS again and look at the title line of the right half of the screen; it includes *C:\BUDGETS*, the path name of the highlighted directory. Press the down arrow key to highlight CHARTS; now the title line on the right includes

C:\BUDGETS\CHARTS. Press the down arrow again to highlight OLD, and the title line includes C:\BUDGETS\CHARTS\OLD.

A directory's full name consists of the letter that identifies the disk drive followed by a colon (in this case, C:), followed by the name of each directory starting with the root directory (whose name, remember, is \) that leads to it; the individual names are separated with a backslash character (\). This series of names is called the *path name* of the directory, or often just the *path*. It gives DOS all the information it needs to find a directory anywhere on the disk.

A Table of Contents for Your Disk

The directory tree serves the same sort of purpose as the table of contents of a book. When you look at the table of contents, you might look at just the chapter titles to get the big picture; if you were looking for something more specific, however, you might look at the major headings beneath each chapter title. Think of your hard disk as the book itself, your directories as chapter titles, and your subdirectories as the major headings; you can use them to look for a particular file on your hard disk just as you would use the table of contents to find a particular passage in a book.

But the directory tree is more versatile than a table of contents, because the Shell lets you control how many levels of the directory structure are displayed. You can display just the directories in the root directory, all the subdirectories in one branch of the directory tree, or all the directories and subdirectories on the disk. This lets you focus your work on just the part of the disk you're interested in.

Branches of the Directory Tree

A branch consists of a directory and all the subdirectories it contains; as you've seen, the Shell represents this structure in the directory tree by offsetting a subdirectory below and to the right of the directory that contains it, connecting the file folder symbols (icons) that precede the directory names with lines that show the relationship.

For example, look at the branch you just created. The icon for BUDGETS is connected to the line coming out the bottom of the root directory, showing you that BUDGETS is contained in the root dircctory. The icons for CHARTS and REPORTS are connected to a line coming out the bottom of the BUDGETS icon, and the icon for OLD is connected to a line coming out the bottom of the CHARTS icon.

Expanding and Collapsing a Branch

Right now, you can see all the directories in the branch that begins with BUDGETS. But this takes up room on the screen that might keep some of the other directories at the same level as BUDGETS from being visible. To eliminate this detail, you can tell the Shell to display just the first directory of the branch; this is called *collapsing* the branch.

Press the up arrow key to highlight CHARTS. The directory tree shows you that CHARTS is the first directory in a branch that contains just one other directory, named OLD. Notice that there's a minus sign inside the icon to the left of CHARTS.

You use the Tree menu to control how many levels of directories are displayed. Press Alt+T to display the Tree menu:

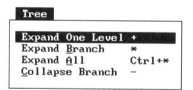

Choose *Collapse Branch* from the Tree menu; the directory named OLD should disappear. The entire branch is represented by the directory that begins it, CHARTS. But look again inside the icon to the left of CHARTS: The minus sign has changed to a plus sign.

Only directories that contain other directories (directories that begin a branch) contain these signs. The minus sign means that the subdirectories contained in the directory are displayed (the first level of the branch is expanded); the plus sign means that the directory contains one or more subdirectories, but they're not shown (the branch is collapsed). If the icon is blank, either the directory is empty or it contains just files.

Working with the directory tree is one instance where using short-cut keys is definitely easier than choosing commands from menus. Display the Tree menu again, and look to the right of the commands; the keys listed there—plus (+), asterisk (*), Control+asterisk (*Ctrl+*), and minus (-)—are the shortcut keys for the corresponding Tree commands. Press Esc to leave the Tree menu.

To see how these commands work, move the highlight up to BUDGETS and press minus (-). CHARTS, OLD, and REPORTS should all disappear, leaving only BUDGETS of the four directories you created; its icon contains a +, telling you that there are more levels of directories not shown.

To expand the first level of the branch, press the plus key (+). CHARTS and REPORTS return to the display; OLD, however, is another level down, so it isn't displayed (the + inside the icon for CHARTS shows that there is at least another level).

You can display all the levels of a branch by pressing * instead of +. Press - to collapse the branch again and now press *. This time, CHARTS, REPORTS, and OLD all reappear. All the icons are either blank or contain a minus sign, telling you that there are no more levels of directories to be displayed.

The Root of All Directories

All the directories on the disk are part of the branch that begins with the root directory, so you should be able to collapse the entire directory tree. Press Home to highlight the root directory (C:\), and press -. Sure enough, the only directory you should see is C:\. Your screen should look like this:

It's just as quick to change the directory tree display using the mouse. To expand the root directory, click on the + in the icon to the left of C:\ instead of pressing +. You should see every directory in the root directory but not the directories they contain; the plus signs in the icons tell you which directories contain more directories (for example, BUDGETS). Clicking the plus and minus signs in these icons has the same effect as pressing + and -.

The plus sign expands the directory tree one level; you can expand every branch of the directory by pressing Ctrl-* (hold down the key labeled *Ctrl* and press *). Try it. The directory tree now should show you all levels of directories, including CHARTS, REPORTS, and OLD, under BUDGETS.

Changing a Directory's Name

If you decide to change the label on a file folder after you've set up a paper filing system, you just erase the name and write the new one or put a new label on the folder. You can accomplish the same thing by changing the name of a directory using the Rename command from the File menu.

Suppose you decide to change the name of the directory OLD to HISTORY. Highlight OLD in the directory tree, then choose *Rename* from the File menu. The Shell displays the Rename Directory dialog box:

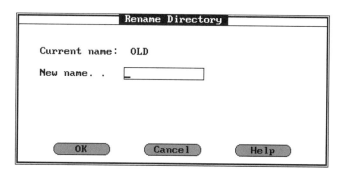

The dialog box tells you that the current name of the directory is OLD, and is prompting you to type the new name. Type history and press Enter. Now the directory in the branch that begins with CHARTS is named HISTORY.

Chapter Review

You should now be able to find your way around the directories and subdirectories on your hard disk. In the next chapter, you'll put some files in the directories you created. The most important points covered in this chapter:

- A computer *file*, like a paper file, contains information that you have saved.

- A *directory* is an area of the disk where files are stored. A directory can also contain other directories, called *subdirectories*.

- You use the Create Directory command from the File menu to add new directories to your hard disk.

- You can name and organize the directories on your disk to suit the way you use your computer.

- You use the Rename command from the File menu to change the name of a directory after you have created it.

- Every disk starts with one directory, called the *root directory*; its name is always the backslash character (\).

  The *file list area* of the Shell screen includes the directory tree on the left and the file list on the right.

- The *directory tree* shows you the names of the directories and how they are structured.

- The *file list* shows you the name, size, and date of last change of each file in the directory highlighted in the directory tree.

- A *branch* of the directory tree consists of a directory and any subdirectories it contains.

- You can *expand* a branch to show the first level of sub-directories by pressing the plus key (+) or clicking the + in the icon that precedes the directory name; to expand all levels of the branch, you press *.

- You can *collapse* a branch to show only the beginning directory by pressing the minus key (-) or clicking the - in the icon that precedes the directory name.

- You can expand the entire directory tree by pressing Ctrl+*.

CHAPTER
3

WORKING WITH FILES

Most of your computer work will involve creating, changing, or deleting files. This is borne out by the nature of the Shell's capabilities: The majority perform some sort of operation on a file (or control the appearance or behavior of the Shell).

This chapter shows you some of the basic file-handling capabilities of the Shell. If you're continuing from Chapter 2 or if you just turned your system on, the title bar of the directory tree should be highlighted (if it isn't, use the Tab key or mouse to highlight it). Highlight the DOS directory in the directory tree, then move to the file list; your screen should look something like this:

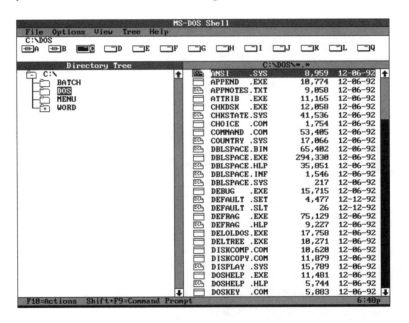

It's not important if the directory tree is a little different, but notice that the *DOS* directory is highlighted and the file list area shows your DOS files. If your screen doesn't look like this, choose *Single File List* from the View menu, highlight the directory named DOS, then move to the file list.

The File Name

Like people, a file has a first name and usually, but not always, a last name. A file's first name can be from one to eight characters long; its last name, called an *extension*, can be up to three characters long. The name and extension are separated by a period. The combination of name, period, and extension is called the file name.

DOS lets you use letters, numbers, and most punctuation marks in a file name. Just as your last name tells other people the family you belong to and perhaps gives a hint as to your heritage, a file's extension often gives a clue about the contents or purpose of a file. DOS enforces a few hard and fast rules about the meaning of certain file extensions. For example, COM and EXE (for *command* and *executable*) mean that a file contains a program, such as WordPerfect or the DOS Shell; SYS (for *system*) means that a file contains either a program or data used only by DOS.

Over the years, other, less formal conventions for file extensions have evolved; for example, HLP (for *help*) usually means that a file contains information that is displayed when you ask a program for help; TXT (for *text*) usually means that a file contains a written document, such as a letter. Some programs use specific extensions to identify the files they create, such as WKS (for *worksheet*) for Lotus 1-2-3, or PM4 for *PageMaker* version *4*.

Files in the same directory can have the same name or the same extension, but not both.

How Big Is a File?

In addition to the file name, the file list shows two other items of information for each file: its size, and the date the file was created or last changed.

The size is given in *bytes*. Byte is one of those computer words you just can't escape. It's a unit of measure, like mile or cubic centimeter, but it measures computer storage (either memory or disk storage) rather than distance or volume. A byte is the amount of storage it takes to store one character (letter, number, or symbol); the text on a page of this book would take up about 2,500 bytes.

If you look down the size column of the file list, you'll see that files can range from quite small to very large. For example, the file named DBLSPACE.SYS near the middle of the list is only a few hundred bytes long, but the file named DBLSPACE.EXE a few lines above is nearly 300,000 bytes long. (Actually, a file can be much longer than this; desktop publishing and data base files, in particular, can run into the millions of bytes).

How Old Is That File?

The date the file was created or last changed is a more useful number than it might seem. For example, look at the date column, the last column on the right. Most dates should be the same, because that's the date that the final version of the DOS files were created before the product was shipped. (A few files will have a more recent date because they change whenever the Shell or some other program is run.)

One of the most common uses of the date is to keep track of different versions of a file. Suppose you're working on a report or spreadsheet and give each version a slightly different name. If the file name variations don't identify the most recent version, the date will tell you which file was worked on most recently.

Copying a File

Just as you use a copy machine to make a copy of a canceled check or utility bill, sometimes you'll want to make a copy of a disk file. You'll want to periodically save copies of your files on floppy disks, for example, or rearrange the filing system on your hard disk.

To use the keyboard to copy a file, you highlight the file, then choose *Copy* from the File menu. For example, suppose you wanted to make a copy of the file named CHOICE.COM in the directory named \DOS—the backslash at the beginning is the *path*, which means that the directory is in the root directory. You want the copy in the directory you created named \BUDGETS. Follow these steps:

1. Highlight the file named CHOICE.COM (it should be near the top of the list).

2. Choose *Copy* from the File menu. The Shell displays the Copy File dialog box:

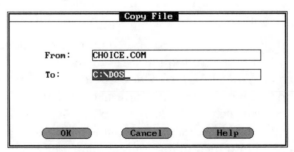

Notice that the name of the file you want to copy is in the *From* box and the name of the directory where it is stored is in the *To* box. The contents of the *To* box are highlighted, indicating that anything you type will replace it.

3. Type \budgets, the name of the directory where you want to store the copy of CHOICE.COM, and press Enter.

When the dialog box disappears, the file has been copied. To confirm, first notice that it still exists in the directory \DOS (it should still be highlighted); now move back to the directory tree and highlight \BUDGETS; the list of files should show CHOICE.COM. Now you've got two copies of the file on your disk; DOS can tell them apart because they're in different directories.

Dragging Files with the Mouse

Although using the mouse for some operations takes about the same amount of time as using the keyboard—maybe even a bit more, especially if you have to take your hand off the keyboard and find the mouse—here's a case where the mouse wins hands down. Instead of highlighting the file, choosing *Copy* from the File menu, and typing the name of the directory where you want the copy of the file, you can use the mouse to simply drag the file to the new directory.

Suppose you want to make another copy of CHOICE.COM in the directory named \BUDGETS\CHARTS. It takes longer to describe how to do it with the mouse than to actually do it. The BUDGETS directory is highlighted; follow these steps:

1. Move the mouse pointer to the file name (CHOICE.COM) in the file list.

2. Press and hold the Ctrl key, press and hold the left mouse button, and slowly move the mouse toward the directory tree.

When the pointer leaves the file name, its shape changes from an arrow to a circle with a diagonal line through it; this represents the international symbol for *not allowed* and means that if you release the mouse button nothing will happen. As the pointer crosses the border that divides the directory tree from the file list, the pointer changes to a duplicate of the icon to the left of the file name. This means that if you release the mouse button now, a copy of the file will be stored in the highlighted directory. Watch the bottom line of the screen; it tells you what happens if you release the button.

3. Continue moving the mouse until the pointer is over CHARTS—note that the bottom line reads *Copy CHOICE .COM to CHARTS*—then release it. The Shell displays the Confirm Mouse Operation dialog box:

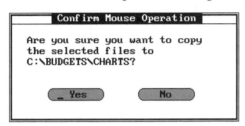

4. Click *Yes* or press Enter.

Now there's a copy of CHOICE.COM in \BUDGETS\ CHARTS, too. To confirm, click on *CHARTS* and check the file list; it should show one file, CHOICE.COM.

Giving a Copy a Different Name

When you told the Shell where to copy the file, you typed just the name of the directory where the copy was to be stored. You can give the copy a different name by typing the new name instead of a directory name.

For example, CHARTS is the highlighted directory; move to the file list and follow these steps to make a copy of the file CHOICE .COM, naming this new copy LETTER1.TXT:

1. Highlight CHOICE.COM.

2. Choose *Copy* from the File menu.

3. When the Shell displays the Copy File dialog box, notice that the *To* box contains the path of the directory you're working in (C:\BUDGETS\CHARTS). Type letter1.txt (the entry disappears when you press the first key) and press Enter.

When the dialog box is cleared, the list of files shows two names: CHOICE.COM and LETTER1.TXT.

You can also make a copy of a file with a different name in a different directory. For example, the steps to make another copy of \BUDGETS\CHARTS\CHOICE.COM, this one named LETTER2 .TXT and in the directory REPORTS, are similar to the steps in the preceding example:

1. Choose *Copy* from the File menu.

2. When the Shell displays the Copy File dialog box, you're going to change the highlighted text in the *To* box instead of replacing it. Press the right arrow key; the name of the directory (C:\BUDGETS\CHARTS) remains, but the highlight goes away, telling you that you can type without replacing the text.

3. Backspace to erase CHARTS and type `reports\letter2 .txt`, but don't press Enter yet. Now the dialog box should look like this:

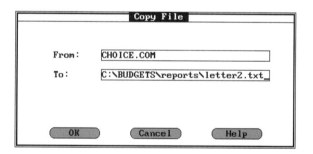

C:\BUDGETS\REPORTS\LETTER2.TXT is the full path name of the file; the path name precisely locates the disk drive and directory where the file is stored and names the file. Notice that the file name at the end is separated from the path (the list of directory names) with a backslash (\), just as the directory names that make up the path are separated with a backslash. You could have named this copy LETTER1.TXT, too, if you wanted, because the files are stored in different directories, so their path names would be different even though their file names are the same.

4. Press Enter.

When the dialog box disappears, highlight the directory
REPORTS; the file list should show LETTER2.TXT.

As you can see, the Shell doesn't give you a chance to type a directory or file name when you drag a file to a new directory. Conse-
quently, if you want to give the copy a different name, you must
choose *Copy* from the File menu.

Moving a File

Moving a file also makes a copy, but the Shell deletes the original file
after it makes the new copy. The procedure differs only slightly from
copying a file: If you're using the keyboard, you select *Move* instead
of *Copy* from the File menu; if you're dragging with the mouse, you
don't hold down the Ctrl key while you drag.

Follow these steps to move the file CHOICE.COM from \BUD-
GETS to \BUDGETS\CHARTS\HISTORY by dragging it:

1. If necessary, expand the branch that begins with CHARTS
   (click the + in the icon to the left of CHARTS or highlight
   CHARTS and press +) to display HISTORY.

2. Highlight the directory named BUDGETS.

3. Move the mouse pointer to CHOICE.COM in the file list (it's
   the only file), press and hold the mouse button—again, notice
   that the pointer changes shape—and drag the file to HIS-
   TORY in the directory tree. Now the bottom line of the screen
   tells you that you're moving the file, not copying it. Release the
   mouse button.

4. When the Shell displays the Confirm Mouse Operation dialog
   box, click *Yes* or press Enter. When the dialog box disappears,
   CHOICE.COM is gone from \BUDGETS (the file list reads
   No files in selected directory).

5. Confirm the move by highlighting the directory named
   HISTORY and checking the file list to confirm that it shows
   CHOICE.COM.

Remember, when you're dragging, you hold down the Ctrl key to copy a file, you don't hold down the Ctrl key to move a file. The Confirm Mouse Operation dialog box tells you whether the file will be moved or copied if you OK the operation.

Selecting More Than One File

What if you want to copy or move two or three files, or more? You could, of course, do each one separately, but if all the files are in the same directory, there's a quicker way: Commands work on all selected files, and the Shell lets you select more than one file.

You can select either a series of several consecutive files in the file list, or several files scattered here and there, using either the keyboard or the mouse. The DOS directory contains plenty of files to practice with, so highlight it. Then highlight the file list.

To highlight several files in a row with the keyboard, you highlight the first file, then hold down the Shift key and use the arrow keys to highlight the files you want. Try it. The first file in the DOS directory should be highlighted; hold down the Shift key and press the down arrow key three times. Now the first four files should be highlighted; the screen should look like this:

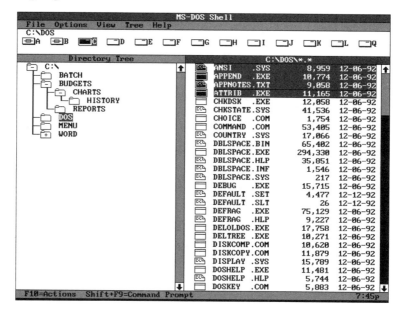

To select several consecutive files using the mouse, you click the first file, hold down the Shift key, and click the last file in the series. For example, suppose you want to select all the files whose name is DBLSPACE. Click the file named DBLSPACE.BIN, hold down the Shift key; then click the file named DBLSPACE.SYS. The Shell should highlight all the files between the two you clicked; the screen should look like this:

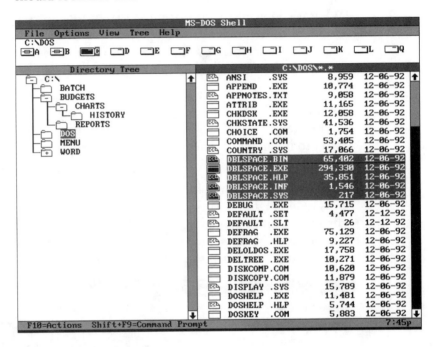

Selecting Files Not in Sequence

To select several files scattered in the file list using the mouse, you click the first file, hold down the Ctrl key, and click the additional files you want. For example, click the file named ANSI.SYS; notice that it is highlighted, and the highlight disappears from all the files named DBLSPACE. Now hold down the Ctrl key, click the files named ATTRIB.EXE and COMMAND.COM, and release the Ctrl key. The Shell highlights just the three files you clicked. The screen should look like this:

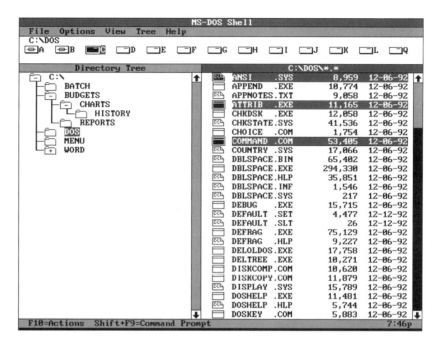

This is another case where the mouse is both simpler and quicker. To select individual files with the keyboard, you highlight the first file, press Shift+F8 to tell the Shell you want to add some files to the selection, highlight the next file using the arrow keys, press the space bar to select the file, then use the arrow keys to highlight the next file, press the space bar again, and continue until you have selected all the files you want; then you press Shift+F8 again to tell the Shell you're through selecting files and finally choose the command you want.

Try it; it really isn't quite as involved as it sounds. To select the same series of three files you just selected with the mouse, use the arrow keys to highlight ANSI.SYS. Now press Shift+F8 and notice that the Shell displays *ADD* toward the right side of the bottom line. Now press the down arrow key to highlight ATTRIB.EXE and press the space bar; press the down arrow key again to highlight COMMAND .COM and press the space bar again. The screen should look the same as the illustration above.

You're going to copy and move several files in the directories that you created, so highlight the directory \BUDGETS\CHARTS (you may have to expand the branch that starts with BUDGETS to see the directory named CHARTS).

Copying a Series of Files

After you have selected several files, copying or moving them works just like copying or moving a single file, except the Shell prompts you to confirm the operation for each file. For example, follow these steps to copy the two files in CHARTS to REPORTS using the keyboard:

1. Select both files (click on CHOICE.COM, hold down the Shift key, and click on LETTER1.TXT).

2. Select *Copy* from the File menu. As before, the Shell displays the Copy File dialog box. You want to store the copies in a different directory, so press the right arrow key, backspace to erase CHARTS, type `reports`, and press Enter.

3. Confirm the copy by highlighting the directory named REPORTS and checking the file list for CHOICE.COM, LETTER1.TXT, and LETTER2.TXT.

Moving a Series of Files

Moving several files works the same way as moving a single file. REPORTS now contains three files; follow these steps to move them all to BUDGETS using the mouse:

1. Select all three files (click on CHOICE.COM, hold down the Shift key, and click on LETTER2.TXT).

2. Click on any highlighted file name and start dragging the mouse toward the directory tree. Notice that when the pointer crosses the border between the file list and directory tree, it changes to a drawing of three sheets of paper to show that you're working with more than one file (and the bottom line tells you that you're going to move, not copy, the files).

3. Move the mouse pointer to BUDGETS and release the button. As before, the Shell displays the Confirm Mouse Operation dialog box. Click *Yes*.

4. Confirm the move by highlighting BUDGETS in the directory tree; the file list should show CHOICE.COM, LETTER1 .TXT, and LETTER2.TXT.

In general, you can perform any operation on as many files as you select.

Deleting Files

As you use your system more, you'll almost certainly start cluttering up your disk with files that you no longer need. This is just an inconvenience until it starts getting difficult to find the file you want in the clutter, or the disk fills and there is no more room for new files. The best way to avoid this situation is to periodically go through your directories and clean house. The Shell makes this chore relatively easy.

As with copying and moving files, deleting one or more files is simply a matter of selecting the files and carrying out the appropriate command—in this case, the Delete command from the File menu.

For example, BUDGETS is highlighted; to delete all the files in it, select all three files. You could choose the Delete command from the File menu, but here's a case where the shortcut key is much quicker and is easy to remember. Press the key marked *Del* or *Delete*; the Shell displays the Delete File dialog box:

The *Delete* box contains the name of each file you selected (it actually contains the names of the last two files and the last part of the first file name, because all three names won't fit in the box). Even when you confirm that you want to delete a file or files, the Shell asks you to confirm each individual deletion before carrying it out; this second chance reduces the likelihood of deleting a file by mistake. Press Enter (or click *OK*) to confirm that you indeed want to delete the files.

Now the Shell displays the Delete File Confirmation dialog box, which specifically asks you to confirm the deletion of the first file, whose full path and file name is C:\BUDGETS\CHOICE.COM:

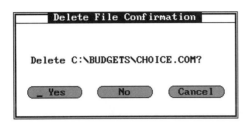

Press Enter to confirm the deletion of CHOICE.COM. Now the Shell prompts you to confirm the deletion of LETTER1.TXT. Press Enter to confirm this deletion, and the next. When the dialog box disappears, the file list once again tells you *No files in selected directory.*

Deleting a Directory

You delete a directory the same way you delete a file: Select the directory to be deleted, then press the Del key (or select *Delete* from the File menu). There's one condition, however; you can't delete a directory unless it's empty—it can't contain any files or other directories.

For example, BUDGETS is highlighted in the directory tree; press Del to delete it. The Shell displays a message box titled *Deletion Error* that tells you that you can't delete a non-empty directory (BUDGETS contains no files, but it does contain two subdirectories —CHARTS and REPORTS). Press Esc to remove the message.

Now highlight \BUDGETS\REPORTS and press Del. This time the Shell displays the Delete Directory Confirmation dialog box:

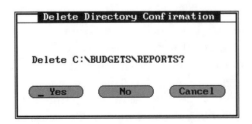

Press Enter (or click *Yes*) to delete the directory. The dialog box disappears and the directory \BUDGETS\REPORTS is gone.

You must delete directories one at a time; the Shell doesn't let you select more than one directory at a time.

Viewing a File

Sometimes you'll want to check what's in a file. The Shell makes it just about as easy as it can get: The View command from the File menu displays the contents of any file. If the file contains ordinary text, you can read it. If the file was created by a word processor, it includes both text and special codes the program uses to control the spacing, font, and other formatting information; you should still be able to pick out the text from the formatting codes.

But if the file contains a program, or data stored in a way that makes sense only to a computer, the screen looks like your computer has gone around the bend. You'll see lots of unfamiliar symbols—perhaps interspersed with occasional letters and numbers—in no apparent order. That's OK, though, mere mortals don't have to understand it; the computer does.

Often the file's extension gives you a hint about its content: Files whose extension is TXT, BAT, or INI usually contain ordinary text; EXE and COM files are programs; DOC files are usually created by word processors. Although the most obvious reason to view a file is to read it, the ability to display any type of file can prove handy.

To see how it works, highlight the file named DOSHELP.HLP in the \DOS directory (you'll have to scroll down a line or two), then choose *View File Contents* from the File menu. The Shell displays the contents of the file:

```
                    MS-DOS Shell - DOSHELP.HLP
  Display  View  Help
 ┌ To view file's content use PgUp or PgDn or ↑ or ↓.                        ┐
 [                                                                            ]
 @ Copyright (C) 1990-1992 Microsoft Corp.  All rights reserved.
 @ This is the DOS general help file.  It contains a brief
 @ description of each command supported by the DOS help command.
 @ Type DOSHELP with no arguments to display the text in this file.
 @ Lines beginning with @ are comments, and are ignored by DOSHELP.
 @ This file may be modified to add new commands.  If the DOSHELP command-name
 @ form is to be used, any new commands should support the /? parameter.
 @ New commands should start in the first column.  Any extra lines needed
 @ for a command description should be preceded by white space.  Commands
 @ must be added in alphabetical order.
 APPEND    Allows programs to open data files in specified directories as if
           they were in the current directory.
 ASSIGN    Redirects requests for disk operations on one drive to a different
           drive.
 ATTRIB    Displays or changes file attributes.
 BREAK     Sets or clears extended CTRL+C checking.
 CALL      Calls one batch program from another.
 CD        Displays the name of or changes the current directory.
 CHCP      Displays or sets the active code page number.
 CHDIR     Displays the name of or changes the current directory.
 CHKDSK    Checks a disk and displays a status report.
 CLS       Clears the screen.
 COMMAND   Starts a new instance of the MS-DOS command interpreter.
 COMP      Compares the contents of two files or sets of files.
 COPY      Copies one or more files to another location.
 CTTY      Changes the terminal device used to control your system.
 DATE      Displays or sets the date.
 DEBUG     Runs Debug, a program testing and editing tool.
 DEL       Deletes one or more files.
 ┌─────────────────────────────────────────────────────────────────────────┐
 └┘=PageDown  Esc=Cancel  F9=Hex/ASCII                              7:58p
```

This screen has only three menus—Display, View, and Help; for all practical purposes, all you can do is look through the file and return to the normal Shell screen. The line below the menu names tells you that you can use the PgUp, PgDn, up arrow, and down arrow keys to scroll through the file. What isn't obvious is that you can click on the *PgUp, PgDn,* and two arrow symbols in that line to accomplish the same thing.

Try it. Click on the down arrow symbol. The display moves one line toward the end of the file. Now hold down the mouse button while the pointer is on the down arrow symbol; the file scrolls continuously a line at a time. Clicking on the *PgDn* in this line (or pressing the PgDn key) moves a full screen toward the end of the file; PgUp moves you a screenful toward the beginning. Pressing the Home key returns you to the beginning of the file.

Press Esc to return to the file list.

To see what a non-text file looks like, highlight the file named APPEND.EXE. Here, again, is a case where the shortcut key is much faster than choosing a command from a menu; to view the file, press F9. The Shell displays something that doesn't appear very helpful:

```
                        MS-DOS Shell - APPEND.EXE
 Display  View  Help
┌ To view file's content use PgUp or PgDn or ↑ or ↓.                          ┐
│                                                                             │
    000000    4D5A1600   16000000   20008A00   FFFF0403    MZ......  .è.  ..
    000010    80000000   10006C02   1E000000   01000000    ç.....l.........
    000020    00000000   00000000   00000000   00000000    ................
    000030    00000000   00000000   00000000   00000000    ................
    000040    00000000   00000000   00000000   00000000    ................
    000050    00000000   00000000   00000000   00000000    ................
    000060    00000000   00000000   00000000   00000000    ................
    000070    00000000   00000000   00000000   00000000    ................
    000080    00000000   00000000   00000000   00000000    ................
    000090    00000000   00000000   00000000   00000000    ................
    0000A0    00000000   00000000   00000000   00000000    ................
    0000B0    00000000   00000000   00000000   00000000    ................
    0000C0    00000000   00000000   00000000   00000000    ................
    0000D0    00000000   00000000   00000000   00000000    ................
    0000E0    00000000   00000000   00000000   00000000    ................
    0000F0    00000000   00000000   00000000   00000000    ................
    000100    00000000   00000000   00000000   00000000    ................
    000110    00000000   00000000   00000000   00000000    ................
    000120    00000000   00000000   00000000   00000000    ................
    000130    00000000   00000000   00000000   00000000    ................
    000140    00000000   00000000   00000000   00000000    ................
    000150    00000000   00000000   00000000   00000000    ................
    000160    00000000   00000000   00000000   00000000    ................
    000170    00000000   00000000   00000000   00000000    ................
    000180    00000000   00000000   00000000   00000000    ................
    000190    00000000   00000000   00000000   00000000    ................
    0001A0    00000000   00000000   00000000   00000000    ................
    0001B0    00000000   00000000   00000000   00000000    ................
    0001C0    00000000   00000000   00000000   00000000    ................
 ←┘=PageDown  Esc=Cancel   F9=Hex/ASCII                                  8:43p
```

This is the beginning of the file named APPEND.EXE, which is a program that carries out a DOS command named Append. The left side of the screen shows the contents of the file as a series of hexadecimal (base 16) numbers; the right side of the screen shows the same portion of the file translated as much as possible into ordinary text. Don't worry if none of this makes sense, it doesn't really have to; this sort of view of a file is most often used by programmers who want to know exactly what is in a file.

To see the more common view of the file, press F9 again—It still looks like a mistake. This is the same view you saw of the previous file; the difference is that the first file contained ordinary text, but this file is a program. Press PgDn, however, and you should see some ordinary text in the middle of the screen.

Scroll through a few screenfuls of the file, and you'll continue to see a mix of ordinary text and odd characters. The ordinary text is the messages that the program displays, and the remainder is the instructions to the computer that makes the program work.

Press Esc to return to the file list.

Chapter Review

This chapter covered a lot of ground fairly quickly. You're well on your way to knowing the Shell, now; you've used most of the Shell's basic file-handling capabilities, and you've had quite a bit of practice using the keyboard and mouse to move around the Shell, selecting files and directories and choosing commands.

The most important points covered in this chapter:

- A DOS *file name* consists of a name of up to 8 characters. It can also include an *extension* of up to 3 characters; the name is separated from the extension by a period.

- A file name can include letters, numbers, and most punctuation and other marks.

- Files are measured in *bytes*. One byte is the amount of storage (either disk or memory) required to store one letter or number.

- The file list shows a file's name, extension, size, and the date the file was created or last changed.

- To *drag* a file, put the mouse pointer on the file name, press and hold the left mouse button, and drag the file name to a different directory.

- Copying a file makes a second copy of the file.

- Moving a file makes a copy in a different directory, then deletes the original.

- When you copy a file to the same directory, you must give it a different name so that DOS can tell the copies apart. When you copy or move a file to a different directory, you can give the new copy a different name or keep the same one.

- To select more than one file in sequence using the keyboard, highlight the first file, hold down the Shift key, and use the arrow keys to select the additional files. To select more than one file using the mouse, click the first file in the sequence, hold down the Shift key, and click the last file in the sequence.

- To select more than one file anywhere in the directory using the mouse, highlight the the first file, hold down the Ctrl key, then click each additional file to be selected. To select more than one file anywhere in the directory using the keyboard, highlight the first file, press Shift+F8, highlight each additional file to be selected, and press the space bar. When you have selected all the files, press Shift+F8 again.

- When you tell the Shell to delete one or more files, it prompts you to confirm each deletion.

- You can't delete a directory that isn't empty (one that contains either files or other directories).

- To view the contents of a file, select the file and press F9 (or choose *View File Contents* from the File menu).

- Files that don't contain ordinary text look like large typographical errors.

CHAPTER

4

WORKING WITH
PROGRAMS

Whenever you're using your computer, DOS is actively at work. Toiling tirelessly but silently in the background, DOS keeps the display, keyboard, disk drives, and other parts of your system running smoothly. The only time you really have to be aware of DOS is when you perform some basic housekeeping task such as copying or deleting a file, formatting a disk, or starting a program.

You have seen how the Shell makes light work of most file management chores; you'll be pleased to know that the Shell makes it just as convenient to run your programs. This chapter shows you several ways to start a program from the Shell. If you're continuing from Chapter 3, your screen should show the directory tree and a file list. For this chapter, add the program list by choosing *Program/File Lists* from the View menu. Your screen should now look like this:

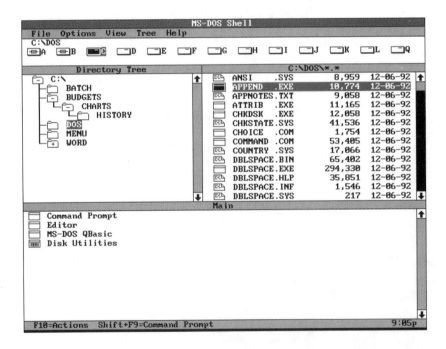

The new area at the bottom of your screen, titled *Main*, is the *program list*, a menu that contains two types of choices: *program items*, which run a program; and *program groups*, which display a different list of choices. You use the program list to organize and work with programs, just as you organize and work with files in the directory tree and file list.

A Menu of Programs—The Program List

Like any other part of the Shell screen, you must move to the program list in order to use it; watch the list of menu names as you click in the program list area or press the Tab key to highlight the title *Main*. Notice that *Tree* disappears from the list of menu names at the top; you don't need its commands when you're using the program list. As you'll see a bit later, the selection of commands in the File menu has also changed.

Unless someone has changed the Shell since it was installed on your computer, the program list displays the following four choices:

The first three choices—*Command Prompt, Editor,* and *MS-DOS QBasic*—are program items; if you choose one of these, the Shell runs the program described by the choice. Notice that the icon preceding these items is an open rectangle with a line near the top, representing a computer screen.

The last item, *Disk Utilities,* is the name of a program group; if you choose it, the Shell displays another list of choices that can include more program items or program groups. Its icon, with the crosshatched area in the middle, represents a keyboard.

Starting a Program from the Program List

You start a program from the program list just as you choose a command from a menu: either double-click on it with the mouse or highlight it and press Enter. Try it; start the DOS Editor by choosing *Editor*. The Shell displays a dialog box titled *File to Edit*:

```
╔══════════════════ File to Edit ══════════════════╗
║                                                    ║
║   Enter the name of the file to edit. To start MS-DOS
║   Editor without opening a file, press ENTER.      ║
║                                                    ║
║   File to edit?    [_                            ] ║
║                                                    ║
║    (   OK   )      (  Cancel  )      (  Help  )    ║
╚════════════════════════════════════════════════════╝
```

When you start the Editor from the program list, this dialog box prompts you for the name of the file you would like to edit; for now, press Enter to start the Editor without opening a file:

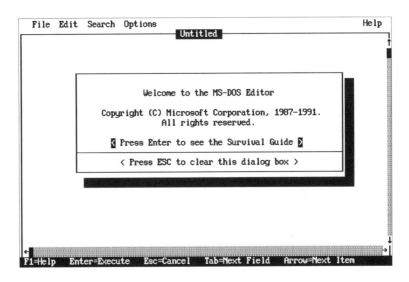

The Editor is useful for creating and editing text files. You'll work with the Editor later in the book: for now, press Esc to remove the notice about the Survival Guide, then leave the Editor by choosing *Exit* from its File menu, just as you would in the Shell.

When you return to the Shell, start the next program by moving the highlight to *MS-DOS QBasic* and pressing Enter. The Shell displays a dialog box similar to the one you saw when you started the Editor, this time asking you to name a QBasic program; press Enter to start QBasic without loading a program, and you might think it's déja vu.

Even though this looks just like the opening screen of the Editor, there is a slight difference; where the Editor opening screen said *Welcome to the MS-DOS Editor*, this one says *Welcome to MS-DOS QBasic*. But otherwise, you're right; they're the same. That's because MS-DOS QBasic includes a text editor that you use to create and revise programs in the Basic language; it looks (and works) just like the DOS Editor.

Return to the Shell by pressing Esc, then choosing *Exit* from the QBasic File menu.

The final program in the Main group, Command Prompt, allows you to temporarily jump back to the DOS prompt without leaving the Shell. Choose *Command Prompt*; the Shell screen goes away and DOS displays the command prompt:

```
Microsoft(R) MS-DOS(R) Version 6.00
            (C)Copyright Microsoft Corp 1981-1993.

C:>
```

This is just like the command prompt you normally see when you run DOS. This choice is handy if you want to run one or two DOS commands and then return to the Shell. To return to the Shell, type `exit` and press Enter.

Running programs from the program list area offers several conveniences. You can place the programs you use often in the Main group, so that they are readily available. If you like, you can create your own dialog boxes that prompt for additional information—just as the DOS Editor and QBasic do—that can be used when starting a program.

Starting a Program from the File List

If you know the name of the file that contains a program, you can start the program from the file list by choosing its file name. You started the Editor a few moments ago by choosing it from the Main program list; now you're going to start it from the file list, so highlight the DOS directory in the directory tree, if necessary. The name of the DOS Editor's program file is EDIT.COM, shown highlighted here (you'll have to scroll down the file list to find it):

```
            C:\DOS\*.*
  DOSSHELL.EXE    236,378   12-06-92  ↑
  DOSSHELL.GRB      4,421   12-06-92
  DOSSHELL.HLP    161,323   12-06-92
  DOSSHELL.INI     17,156   01-03-93
  DOSSHELL.VID      9,462   12-06-92
  DOSSWAP .EXE     18,756   12-06-92
  DRIVER  .SYS      5,406   12-06-92
  EDIT    .COM        413   12-06-92
  EDIT    .HLP     17,898   12-06-92
  EGA     .CPI     58,870   12-06-92
  EGA     .SYS      4,885   12-06-92
  EMM386  .EXE    114,782   12-06-92
  EXPAND  .EXE     16,129   12-06-92
  FASTOPEN.EXE     12,034   12-06-92  ↓
```

To start the Editor, choose EDIT.COM from the file list, just as you would choose a command from a menu.

When you started the Editor from the program list, the Shell displayed a dialog box asking you for the name of a file to edit. This time, however, the opening Editor screen is displayed without displaying that dialog box. Starting a program from the file list gives you much less control over how the program is started; if you use a program often, it's probably worth taking the time to add it to the program list, to make it easier to find and to gain this additional level of control.

Leave the Editor by pressing Esc and then choosing *Exit* from the File menu. After the Editor screen disappears, you're prompted to press any key to return to the Shell. When you press a key, the Shell screen returns, just as it was when you left it. When you add programs to the program list, you can specify that this pause be eliminated.

One other way of starting a program from the file list can be handy if you usually use the same program to work with files that have a specific extension, such as a word processor and files whose extension is DOC.

Starting a Program Automatically

The Associate command on the File menu links a file extension to a program, telling the Shell to start the program whenever you choose a file with that extension. For example, if the word processor you use adds the extension DOC to the files it creates, you could associate the extension DOC with the word processing program; from then on, whenever you chose a file with the extension DOC, the Shell would start your word processor and load the highlighted file.

You can either link a program file to one or more extensions, or link any file with a particular extension to a program file. The Shell prompts you for the pertinent information, depending on what file is highlighted when you choose *Associate*.

Follow these steps to associate the extension TXT (these files usually contain ordinary text) with the DOS Editor, EDIT.COM:

1. Highlight README.TXT in the DOS directory (it's toward the end on the list, so you'll have to scroll):

```
                  C:\DOS\*.*
    PRINT    .EXE       15,640    12-06-92  ↑
    QBASIC   .EXE      194,319    12-06-92
    QBASIC   .HLP      130,810    12-06-92
    RAMDRIVE .SYS        5,873    12-06-92
    README   .TXT       42,618    12-06-92
    REPLACE  .EXE       20,226    12-06-92
    RESTORE  .EXE       38,294    12-06-92
    SETVER   .EXE       12,015    12-12-92
    SHARE    .EXE       10,912    12-06-92
    SIZER    .EXE        6,609    12-06-92
    SMARTDRV .EXE       42,073    12-06-92
    SMARTMON .EXE       28,672    12-06-92
    SMARTMON .HLP       10,727    12-06-92
    SORT     .EXE        6,922    12-06-92  ↓
```

2. Choose *Associate* from the File menu. The Shell displays the Associate File dialog box:

```
┌──────────── Associate File ────────────┐
│                                         │
│                                         │
│  '.TXT' files are associated with:      │
│                                         │
│ ┌─────────────────────────────────────┐│
│ │EDIT                                  ││
│ └─────────────────────────────────────┘│
│                                         │
│                                         │
│                                         │
│                                         │
│                                         │
│    ( OK )      ( Cancel )      ( Help ) │
│                                         │
└─────────────────────────────────────────┘
```

3. Type `c:\dos\edit.com` and press Enter. (Don't worry if something is already filled in the text box. Your typing will erase it.)

    To check out the link, choose README.TXT. The DOS Editor should appear, displaying the first screenful of README .TXT. Choose *Exit* from the File menu to leave the Editor (followed by any key to return to the DOS Shell).

Associating Several Extensions with One Program

Pretty slick. But what if you wanted to associate several extensions with one program? Instead of repeating this process several times, the Shell lets you link several extensions with a program file. You've already linked the extension TXT to the DOS Editor so that you can edit any TXT file simply by choosing it; suppose you wanted to be able to edit files whose extension is HLP and INI the same way. Follow these steps:

1. Highlight the file EDIT.COM in the DOS directory.

2. Choose *Associate* from the File menu. Because a program file is highlighted, the Shell displays a different Associate File dialog box:

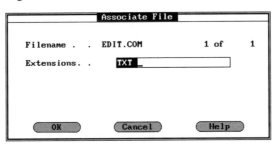

The Associate File dialog box that appeared when you chose *Associate* with README.TXT highlighted asked you the name of the program file to associate with the extension TXT. But here the Shell shows you the name of the file that is highlighted (*EDIT.COM*) and asks you to enter the extensions to be associated with the file. Notice that *TXT* is already entered, because you previously associated README.TXT—meaning all files whose extension is TXT—with EDIT.COM.

3. Press the right arrow key to remove the highlight from the *Extensions* field, so that you can add to the entry without erasing what's already there.

4. To add the extensions HLP and INI, type the following and press Enter:

```
hlp ini
```

That's all there is to it. Now if you choose any file whose extension is TXT, HLP, or INI, the Shell starts the DOS Editor and loads the file you chose.

Overriding an Association

Linking an extension to a program can be handy, but what if you want to load a file with that extension into a different program? For example, you may want to edit a file whose extension is TXT with your word processor rather than the DOS Editor. The Shell gives you three ways to do that:

- Start the program by choosing it from the program list or choosing its file name from the file list, then load the file using the program's commands.

- Choose *Run* from the File menu, then enter the name of the program file followed by the name of the file to be loaded.

- Using the mouse, drag the file to the program.

A bit of explanation of that last item may be in order.

Dragging a File to a Program

You can start a program by clicking and holding the left mouse button on any file name, dragging the resulting icon to the file name of the program you want to start, and releasing the mouse button. This starts the program and, if possible, loads the file you dragged over there.

For example, follow these steps to start EDIT.COM and load the file DOSHELP.HLP:

1. The DOS files are displayed in the file list; move the mouse pointer to DOSHELP.HLP and press and hold the left mouse button (just like when you were copying and moving files in Chapter 3); now move the mouse pointer down to EDIT .COM. (If EDIT.COM isn't visible, you can scroll the list down by dragging the icon over the arrow at the bottom of the scroll bar at the right edge of the file list area.) When you reach EDIT.COM, the message at the bottom of the screen tells you *Start EDIT.COM using DOSHELP.HLP.*

Release the mouse button; the Shell asks you to confirm your request:

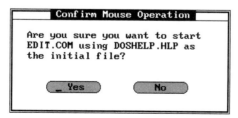

2. Click *Yes* (or press Enter) to start the Editor; it should display the first screenful of DOSHELP.HLP.

3. Choose *Exit* from the File menu and press any key to leave the Editor.

Choosing a Program Group

If you add several programs to the program list, you'll probably want to organize them into groups rather than putting them in one long list. This is much like arranging files in different directories so that you can more easily find the one you want.

The final entry in the Main group is *Disk Utilities*. Notice that the icon to its left is different from the others, identifying it as a program group rather than a program. This group contains several programs—actually, DOS commands—that are frequently used when working with disks. Choose *Disk Utilities*; the Shell replaces the Main group in the program list area with the Disk Utilities group:

Now the first item in the program list is *Main*, whose icon identifies it as a group; this choice returns you to the Main group you just left (you can also return by pressing Esc). The remaining choices perform various disk-management tasks. You won't need these for a while, so choose *Main* to return to the Main group.

As you'll see later in the book, you can create your own program groups; you can also change the Main program group by adding other programs and groups to it or deleting the programs and group currently in it. The only special thing about the Main program group is that you can't delete it; you can delete everything in it, but you can't delete the group itself.

Chapter Review

As you saw in this chapter, running a program from the Shell is as simple as choosing a command from a menu. The main points covered:

- The *program list* is a menu from which you choose program items and program groups.

- A *program item* represents a program that you can run from the Shell.

- A *program group* represents another list of programs and groups that you can display; just as a directory can contain both files and other directories, a program group can contain both program items and other program groups.

- You start a program from the program list by choosing the name of the program item.

- You start a program from the file list by choosing the name of its program file.

- The *Command Prompt* program item temporarily leaves the Shell and lets you type DOS commands directly.

- The *Editor* program item runs the DOS Editor, which lets you create or revise files of text.

- The *MS-DOS QBasic* program item runs QBasic, which lets you create or revise programs written in the QBasic language.

- The *Disk Utilities* program group contains several program items that run DOS commands for managing disks.

- If you *associate* a file extension (such as TXT) with a program, the Shell starts the program whenever you choose a file with that extension.

CHAPTER
5

MANAGING YOUR FILES
WITH THE DOS SHELL

You'll use DOS to manage your files more than for any other purpose. In Chapter 3 you saw most of the routine housekeeping chores,
such as copying, moving, deleting, and viewing the contents of files.
In this chapter you'll tailor the way the Shell organizes the file list and
how it responds to some of your instructions.

If you're continuing from Chapter 4, your screen should be displaying both the file and program list areas, showing the files in the
DOS directory. You won't need the program list in this chapter, so
choose *Single File List* from the View menu to display more of the
file list. Your screen should look like this:

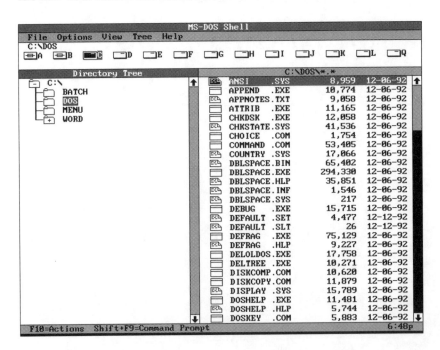

Controlling How the Shell Organizes Your File List

The file list displays the names of the files in alphabetical order.
Right now it should be showing the files in the DOS directory; if
it isn't, highlight DOS in the directory tree so the screen looks like
the preceding illustration.

There will be times when it would be useful to list some of your
files, rather than all of them, or to arrange the names in a different

order. The File Display Options command in the Options menu lets you control which file names are displayed and the order in which they're displayed. Choose *File Display Options* from the Options menu; the Shell displays the File Display Options dialog box:

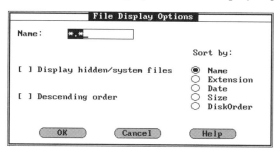

The options in this dialog box control which file names the Shell includes in the list and the order in which the names are listed.

Controlling Which File Names Are Displayed

The entry in the *Name* box specifies which files are to be displayed. If you entered a complete file name—DOSSHELL.HLP, for example—the file list would show just that file (if a file with that name existed). This isn't especially useful; even though it confirms the existence of a particular file, it would probably be just as easy to scroll through the file list.

But there are more useful ways to display the file names. For example, what about displaying all files whose name is DOSSHELL? Type dosshell.* (that's a period and an asterisk following DOS-SHELL); now the *Name* field should look like this:

```
┌══════════ File Display Options ══════════┐
│                                           │
│  Name:      dosshell.*_                   │
│                                           │
│                          Sort by:         │
│                                           │
│  [ ] Display hidden/system files  ● Name  │
│                                   ○ Extension │
│                                   ○ Date  │
│  [ ] Descending order             ○ Size  │
│                                   ○ DiskOrder │
│                                           │
│    ( OK )      ( Cancel )      ( Help )    │
└═══════════════════════════════════════════┘
```

The asterisk is called a *wildcard character*; it represents any character or characters that can be used in a file name. DOSSHELL.*, then, means any file whose name is DOSSHELL, no matter what its extension. Press Enter to see the effect on the file list; the Shell lists each file whose name is DOSSHELL:

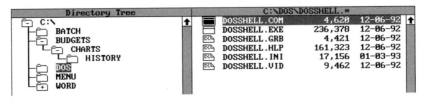

You should see six file names, starting with DOSSHELL.COM and ending with DOSSHELL.VID.

You can use the asterisk to represent an entire extension (as you just did), or an entire file name, or some portion of either a file name or extension. For example, suppose you wanted to quickly locate all help files in the DOS directory. Choose *File Display Options* and type *.hlp in the *Name* field. When you press Enter, the Shell lists all files whose extension is HLP:

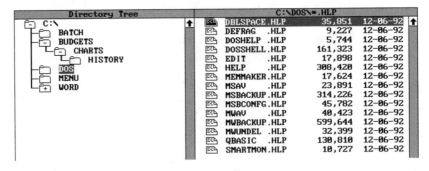

You can see that there are a number of help files in the DOS directory.

Now try using a wildcard to replace part of a file name: choose *File Display Options* again and enter d*.* in the *Name* box to list all files whose name starts with the letter D. When you press Enter, the Shell lists a screenful of files:

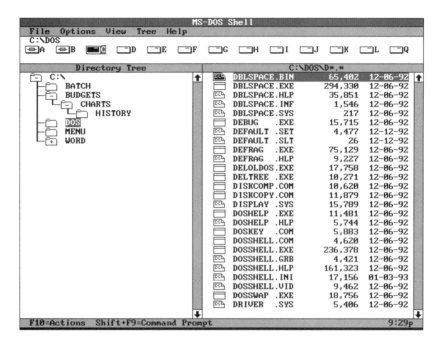

A second wildcard character, the question mark (?), replaces a single character rather than a series of characters. LETTER?.TXT, for example, would represent LETTER1.TXT, LETTER9.TXT, or LETTERS.TXT.

Choose *File Display Options* one more time and type *.* in the *Name* field, restoring it to its original value; this matches all file names and all extensions—in other words, it tells the Shell to list each file in the directory.

A-to-Z or Z-to-A?

Unless you specify otherwise, the Shell displays the file names in alphabetical order from A to Z (numbers precede letters in the sequence). You can reverse this order, listing the files from Z to A (numbers at the end); again, choose *File Display Options* from the Options menu. When the Shell displays the File Display Options dialog box, choose the *Descending order* option either by pressing the Tab key twice and then the space bar, or by clicking anywhere in the brackets or name of the option. Now press Enter; the Shell displays the files starting with the end of the alphabet:

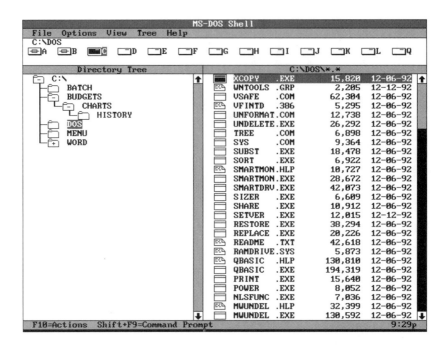

Now the list of file names starts with XCOPY.EXE, which used to be last in the list.

Listing Files by Size

If you're looking for a particular file or group of files by name, having the file names in alphabetical order makes it much easier to find. But sometimes a file's name isn't as important to you as its extension, or size, or the date it was created or last modified. The Shell lets you organize the list of file names by any of the characteristics described in the four columns of information that follow each file name: name, extension, size, and date. (You can also, if you wish, list the files in the same order in which they're actually stored on the disk).

For example, suppose you're interested in all files with a particular extension. To list the files by extension, choose *File Display Options* from the Options menu, change the *Sort by* option to *Extension*, and turn off the *Descending order* option. When you press Enter, the Shell displays the file names with like extensions grouped together:

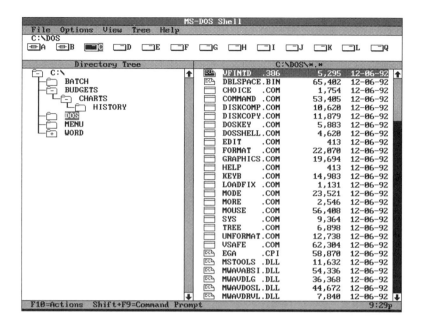

Suppose you were looking for the largest files in a directory. You don't have to scroll through the file list trying to find it; choose *File Display Options* from the Options menu, turn on *Descending order*, and specify *Size* for the *Sort by* option.

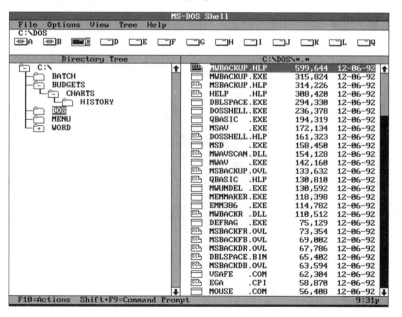

The resulting list displays all the files in the directory, from the largest at the top to the smallest at the bottom. Choose *File Display Options* one last time and restore the usual condition by turning off *Descending order* and setting *Sort by* to *Name*.

Displaying Hidden Files

DOS—and a few other programs—sometimes stores files on your disk whose names aren't normally displayed either by the Shell in the file list or by the Dir[ectory] command when you type it at the DOS prompt. The Display Hidden Files command from the Options menu lets you include these files in the list; when their names are displayed, however, you can also move or delete them, which could cause your system to behave erratically, or not even run at all. Unless you have a reason to deal with specific hidden files on your disk, you should leave this option off.

Finding a File Anywhere on Your Disk

It's amazing how fast files accumulate on a hard disk. It's not at all unusual for a disk to hold hundreds, even thousands of files. This can make it tough to find the file you want. Sometimes you can remember the name of a file but not the directory where you stored it; sometimes you'd just like to see the names of all the files on your hard disk with a particular name or extension. The DOS Shell offers a quick solution: the Search command from the File menu.

Choose *Search* from the File menu; the Shell displays the Search File dialog box:

You enter the name of the file you're looking for in the *Search for* field; you can use the wildcard characters * and ? just as you did in the File Display Options dialog box to search for all the files with similar names or extensions. If the *Search entire disk* box is checked, the Shell searches all directories on the hard disk; if it isn't checked, only the current directory is searched.

For example, to display the names of all files on your hard disk whose extension is TXT, type *.txt in the *Search for* field, leave the *Search entire disk* option on (it should have an X in front of it), and click *OK* or press Enter:

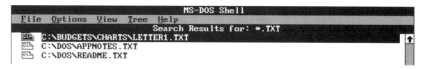

It's difficult to predict exactly what file names you'll see but, at a minimum, the list should include APPNOTES.TXT and READ ME.TXT from the DOS directory and LETTER1.TXT from BUDGETS\CHARTS. Although the files listed may be scattered all over your hard disk, you can work with them just as you would in the normal file list, using the commands from the File menu to copy, move, or delete them, or for viewing their contents.

Press Esc to clear the list from the screen.

Changing a File's Name

Just like paper files, disk files proliferate. No matter how tidy you are, you'll find yourself periodically pruning and reorganizing, getting rid of files you no longer need, adding new directories and deleting others. Sometimes you won't want to delete a file or directory, you'll just want to change its name. That's why the File menu includes the Rename command.

To try the Rename command, you'll change the name of the directory named BUDGETS that you created in Chapter 2 to ACCOUNTS. Highlight BUDGETS, then choose *Rename* from the File menu. The Shell displays the Rename Directory dialog box:

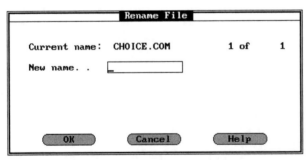

The name of the highlighted directory is shown in the *Current name* field: type accounts and press Enter. Now check the directory tree; there's no directory named BUDGETS, but there is a directory named ACCOUNTS near the top. Highlight ACCOUNTS.

You can rename a file just as easily. Expand the ACCOUNTS directory (it contains the same subdirectories as BUDGETS did) and highlight CHARTS. This directory should contain two files: CHOICE.COM and LETTER1.TXT. Highlight CHOICE.COM and choose *Rename* from the File menu. The Shell displays the Rename File dialog box:

Type letter2.txt and press Enter. Now you have files named LETTER1.TXT and LETTER2.TXT.

If you want to rename several files, you don't have to highlight and rename each one in turn. You can highlight them all at once; the Shell prompts you to rename each one. Try it by renaming the files in CHARTS; highlight both LETTER1.TXT and LETTER2 .TXT (hold down the Shift key and press Up or Down arrow, or hold down Ctrl and click on both files), then choose *Rename* from the File menu; once more the Shell displays the Rename File dialog box, but this time it says *1 of 2* at the upper right:

```
┌──────────────────■ Rename File ■──────────────────┐
│                                                    │
│   Current name:  LETTER1.TXT        1 of      2    │
│                                                    │
│   New name. .     [_                          ]    │
│                                                    │
│                                                    │
│                                                    │
│    ( ▁ OK ▁ )       ( Cancel )       ( Help )      │
│                                                    │
└────────────────────────────────────────────────────┘
```

Type `memo1.txt` as the new name for LETTER1.TXT and press Enter. The dialog box is replaced by dialog box 2 of 2, which shows *LETTER2.TXT* as the current name. Type `memo2.txt` and press Enter. Now the file list should show two files in CHARTS named MEMO1.TXT and MEMO2.TXT.

Protecting Yourself against Pilot Error

Several times during the examples in the book the Shell has displayed a dialog box asking you to confirm deleting a file or using the mouse to move or copy a file. If you were to highlight MEMO1 .TXT and press Del, for example, the Shell would display the Delete File Confirmation dialog box:

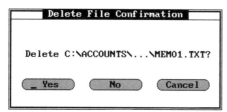

```
┌────────■ Delete File Confirmation ■────────┐
│                                             │
│   Delete C:\ACCOUNTS\...\MEMO1.TXT?         │
│                                             │
│   ( ▁ Yes )     (  No  )     ( Cancel )     │
│                                             │
└─────────────────────────────────────────────┘
```

This gives you a chance to reconsider an action that might destroy some valuable information. Most people welcome this short safety reminder, but if it annoys you, you can turn it off. Choose *Confirmation* from the Options menu to see the three sorts of confirmation the Shell offers:

```
┌────────────■ Confirmation ■────────────┐
│                                         │
│   [X] Confirm on Delete                 │
│   [X] Confirm on Replace                │
│   [X] Confirm on Mouse Operation        │
│                                         │
│                                         │
│   ( ▁ OK ▁ )   ( ▁Cancel )   ( Help )   │
│                                         │
└─────────────────────────────────────────┘
```

All of the options should currently be checked in your dialog box, meaning that deleting a file, replacing a file (making a copy of a file that has the same name as another file), or using the mouse to copy or move a file will generate a request for confirmation. If any options are not checked, turn them on and then press Enter to close this dialog box. A few brief examples show the effect of these options:

1. Copy MEMO1.TXT from the directory named CHARTS to its subdirectory HISTORY. First, highlight CHARTS if necessary. If you have a mouse, hold the Ctrl key down while you drag MEMO1.TXT to HISTORY. The Shell displays the Confirm Mouse Action dialog box:

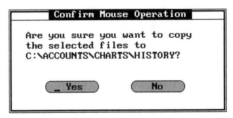

Confirm the copy by clicking on *Yes*.

If you don't have a mouse, highlight MEMO1.TXT, choose *Copy* from the File menu, type `history\memo1.txt` in the *To* field, and press Enter.

2. Repeat step 1 to copy MEMO1.TXT into the HISTORY directory again. This time, after displaying the Confirm Mouse Operation dialog box (press Enter or click on *OK* to confirm the copy), the Shell displays the Replace File Confirmation dialog box because you're telling the Shell to copy a file on top of another file with the same name:

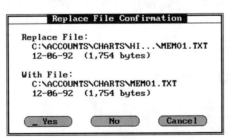

The Shell asks you to confirm this because the operation re-places the existing file named MEMO1.TXT in HISTORY with the new file you copied in. In this instance you're copying the same file, so nothing will be lost, but it's possible to have different files with the same name. If you copy a file with the same name but different contents as an existing file, the exist-ing file is lost; this could mean losing valuable information, so the Shell gives you a chance to reconsider.

Click on *Yes* to confirm this copy, too.

3. With MEMO1.TXT still selected, press the Del key. The Shell displays yet another dialog box named Delete File Confirma-tion. Press Enter to delete MEMO1.TXT from CHARTS.

Now choose *Confirmation* again from the Options menu, turn all three options off, and press Enter. Repeat the previous three steps, using MEMO2.TXT in place of MEMO1.TXT. The Shell carries out all the operations with no confirmation. Turning off confirma-tion can speed things up, but it can also get you into trouble a lot faster.

Choose *Confirmation* from the Options menu and turn all three options back on. Until you think you're ready to work without a net, it's a good idea to give yourself this second chance. If you're bound and determined to speed things up, turn off *Confirmation on Mouse Operation* but leave the other two on; inadvertently deleting just one file can cost you more grief than dozens or hundreds of brief delays.

Chapter Review

The techniques you saw in this chapter let you organize the file list however you like; you should be able to locate quickly any file or group of related files on your hard disk. The major points covered:

* Files are normally listed in ascending alphabetical order (A to Z) according to the standard setting of the File Display Op-tions command in the Options menu.

* The Descending Order option of the File Display Options command lists the file names in descending alphabetical order (Z to A).

- The Sort By option of the File Display Options command controls the order in which file names are listed.

- The wildcard characters * and ? let you work with groups of files with similar names or extensions. The * represents any number of characters in a name or extension. The ? represents a single character.

- Hidden files don't normally appear in the file list. You can include these hidden files by turning on the Display Hidden option of the File Display Options command, but you should do that only to work with specific hidden files, then turn the option off again, to avoid moving or deleting hidden files that DOS or other programs need.

- The Search command in the File menu locates a file or group of files with similar names or extensions anywhere on your hard disk.

- The Rename command in the File menu changes the name of a directory, a file, or a group of files.

- You can control whether the Shell displays a confirmation dialog box every time you delete a file, replace a file, or use the mouse to copy or move a file.

CHAPTER
6

TAILORING THE
PROGRAM LIST

The program groups that come with the Shell—Main and Disk Utilities—are useful, but they certainly don't contain all the programs you'll want to use. The Shell lets you add your own programs to the program list, either as a choice in the Main group or in other groups that you create. You'll do that in this chapter, plus delete a program from a program group and create your own dialog box that prompts for information about how to start a program.

If you're continuing from Chapter 5, your screen should show the directory tree and file list. You're going to work with both the program list and the file list in this chapter, so, if necessary, choose *Program/File Lists* from the View menu. The screen should look like this:

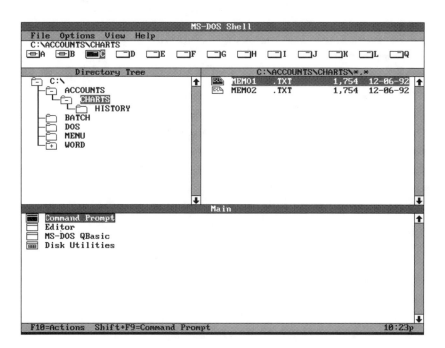

Creating a New Group

Creating a new group is easy. Follow these steps to create a group named DOS Group in the Main group:

1. Highlight *Main* at the top of the program list and choose *New* from the File menu. The Shell displays the New Program Object dialog box:

```
╔══════════════ New Program Object ══════════════╗
║  ┌─ New ──────────────────                      ║
║  │  ○ Program Group          (    OK    )        ║
║  │                                               ║
║  │  ● Program Item           (  Cancel  )        ║
║  └───────────────────                            ║
╚════════════════════════════════════════════════╝
```

2. The New command lets you either add a program to a group or create a new group. Press Up arrow, then Enter, to select *Program Group*. Now the Shell displays the Add Group dialog box:

```
╔══════════════════ Add Group ══════════════════╗
║   Required                                      ║
║     Title  .  .  .  .    [_              ]       ║
║   Optional                                      ║
║     Help Text  .  .      [              ]        ║
║     Password   .  .      [            ]          ║
║                                                 ║
║     (   OK   )    ( Cancel )    ( Help )         ║
╚═════════════════════════════════════════════════╝
```

3. The Shell is waiting for you to type the title that you want to appear in the program list (such as *Command Prompt* or *MS-DOS QBasic*). Type the following, but don't press Enter yet:

```
DOS Group
```

4. Tab to the *Help Text* field. This entry isn't required; it specifies what the Shell displays if you press F1 (the Help key) when the group name is highlighted. Type the following, pressing Enter only at the end:

```
This program group contains the DOS Editor and
QBasic. I added it to personalize the Shell.
```

Now the program list shows a new group at the end, called *DOS Group*.

Before you add some programs to the new group, check out your help message by highlighting *DOS Group* and pressing F1. The Shell displays a window titled *MS-DOS Shell Help* and subtitled *Help for DOS Group*; it contains your help message:

Your help message is displayed just like the help messages for the regular Shell commands. You could have entered a help message of up to 255 characters. Press Esc to clear the Help dialog box.

Adding a Program to a Group

To add programs to a group, the group must be displayed, so press Enter to choose DOS group. The program list now is titled *DOS Group*, but the only entry is *Main*, which just returns you to the Main group you just left. You're going to add two program items, the DOS Editor and QBasic. Follow these steps to add the DOS Editor:

1. Choose *New* from the File menu; the Shell displays the same New Program Object dialog box you saw when you added DOS Group a bit ago.

2. Press Enter to add a program item (remember, the Shell refers to an individual program as a *program item*). The Shell displays the Add Program dialog box:

```
┌──────────────────── Add Program ────────────────────┐
│                                                      │
│  Program Title . . . .  [_                         ] │
│                                                      │
│  Commands  . . . . . .  [                          ] │
│                                                      │
│  Startup Directory . .  [                          ] │
│                                                      │
│  Application Shortcut Key        [                ]  │
│                                                      │
│  [X] Pause after exit        Password . .  [       ] │
│       ( OK )    ( Cancel )    ( Help )   ( Advanced... ) │
└──────────────────────────────────────────────────────┘
```

3. The cursor is in the *Program Title* field; this is where you specify the name of the item that will be displayed as a choice in the QBasic Games group. Type `DOS Editor` and press Tab to move to the *Commands* field.

4. The *Commands* field is where you enter the actual command required to start the program. Type the following (but don't press Enter yet):

       edit

5. The rest of the entries are optional, but press Tab to move to the next field, titled *Startup Directory*. This is where you can tell the Shell which directory contains the program. The Editor program is in the directory named \DOS, so type `\dos` (don't forget the backslash).

The dialog box should look like this:

```
┌──────────────────── Add Program ────────────────────┐
│                                                      │
│  Program Title . . . .  [DOS Editor               ] │
│                                                      │
│  Commands  . . . . . .  [edit                      ] │
│                                                      │
│  Startup Directory . .  [\dos_                     ] │
│                                                      │
│  Application Shortcut Key        [                ]  │
│                                                      │
│  [X] Pause after exit        Password . .  [       ] │
│       ( OK )    ( Cancel )    ( Help )   ( Advanced... ) │
└──────────────────────────────────────────────────────┘
```

6. Press Enter to complete adding the program item.

The DOS Group shows two items: *Main* and *DOS Editor.* Add one more item to this group by repeating the previous steps, substituting *QBasic* for *DOS Editor* in step 3, then substituting *qbasic* for *edit* in step 4. Now the DOS Group should show three choices:

These program items have the same effect as the choices *Editor* and *MSDOS QBasic* in the Main program group. They were chosen because you would be able to follow the examples (you're bound to have the DOS program files), not because they're particularly useful. You would follow the same procedure to create your own program groups and add your own application programs.

Deleting a Program Item

To delete a program from a group, you highlight it and press the Del key (the shortcut for choosing *Delete* from the File menu). Deleting a program from a group doesn't delete the program file from your hard disk, it simply removes the program as an entry in the menu of choices presented by the program group.

To delete QBasic from the DOS Group, highlight *QBasic* and press Del. When the Shell displays the Delete Item dialog box, press Enter. Now the DOS Group shows only two choices, *Main* and *DOS Editor*.

Press Esc to return to the Main group.

Creating Your Own Dialog Box

You added a new group and some programs to the program list, you deleted one program from a program group, and you even wrote your own help message. The programs you added were part of DOS, but they could just as easily have been programs that you use. These tools are enough to let you tailor the Shell to your specific needs.

There's one more thing you can do that gives you more control over how the Shell starts a program: You can have the Shell display a dialog box that prompts for a specific item of information before running a program. Do you recall that the Shell prompts you to enter the name of a file to edit before it starts the Editor? As a reminder, choose *Editor from the Main group*; the Shell displays the File to Edit dialog box:

```
┌──────────────────── File to Edit ────────────────────┐
│                                                       │
│  Enter the name of the file to edit. To start MS-DOS  │
│  Editor without opening a file, press ENTER.          │
│                                                       │
│  File to edit?        ┌─────────────────────────────┐ │
│                       │_                            │ │
│                       └─────────────────────────────┘ │
│     ▄▄▄▄▄▄▄▄          ▄▄▄▄▄▄▄▄▄▄          ▄▄▄▄▄▄▄▄▄▄   │
│    (   OK   )        (  Cancel  )        (  Help  )   │
│     ▀▀▀▀▀▀▀▀          ▀▀▀▀▀▀▀▀▀▀          ▀▀▀▀▀▀▀▀▀▀   │
└───────────────────────────────────────────────────────┘
```

You can create the same sort of dialog box for the programs that you add to the program list. To see how the File to Edit dialog box was created, you'll look at how the Shell defines the Editor program item. Press Esc to clear the dialog box.

Programs Have Properties

When you used the New command to add a program to the QBasic Games group, the Shell displayed a dialog box in which you entered the title to be displayed and the command required to start the program. The Shell calls these pieces of information *properties*; you can change the way a program item or program group looks or behaves by changing its properties.

To see how the Editor's File to Edit dialog box is defined, look at the properties associated with the Editor by highlighting *Editor* in the program list, then choosing *Properties* from the File menu. The Shell displays the Program Item Properties dialog box:

```
┌──────────────────── Program Item Properties ────────────────────┐
│                                                                  │
│  Program Title . . . .  ┌─────────────────────────────────────┐  │
│                         │Editor_                              │  │
│                         └─────────────────────────────────────┘  │
│  Commands  . . . . . .  ┌─────────────────────────────────────┐  │
│                         │EDIT %1                              │  │
│                         └─────────────────────────────────────┘  │
│  Startup Directory . .  ┌─────────────────────────────────────┐  │
│                         │                                     │  │
│                         └─────────────────────────────────────┘  │
│  Application Shortcut Key  ┌──────────────────────────────────┐  │
│                            │                                  │  │
│                            └──────────────────────────────────┘  │
│  [ ] Pause after exit       Password . .  ┌───────────────────┐  │
│                                           │                   │  │
│                                           └───────────────────┘  │
│   ▄▄▄▄▄▄▄▄    ▄▄▄▄▄▄▄▄▄▄     ▄▄▄▄▄▄▄▄     ▄▄▄▄▄▄▄▄▄▄▄▄▄        │
│  (   OK   )  (  Cancel  )   (  Help  )   ( Advanced... )       │
│   ▀▀▀▀▀▀▀▀    ▀▀▀▀▀▀▀▀▀▀     ▀▀▀▀▀▀▀▀     ▀▀▀▀▀▀▀▀▀▀▀▀▀        │
└──────────────────────────────────────────────────────────────────┘
```

Notice the entry in the *Commands* field: C:\DOS\EDIT starts EDIT.COM in the DOS directory, but what does %1 do? It tells the Shell to display a dialog box that asks for more information; this is how you create a dialog box. When you press Enter or choose *OK* with this dialog box on the screen and *%1* in the *Commands* field, the Shell displays another dialog box that asks you to specify the title and other properties of the dialog box that is to be displayed.

Press Enter; the Shell displays a second Program Item Properties dialog box that shows how the File to Edit dialog box is defined:

```
┌────────────────── Program Item Properties ──────────────────┐
│                                                              │
│  Fill in information for % 1   prompt dialog.                │
│                                                              │
│  Window Title  . . . .   [File to Edit_            ]         │
│                                                              │
│  Program Information .    [out opening a file, press ENTER.] │
│                                                              │
│  Prompt Message  . . .    [File to edit?          ]          │
│                                                              │
│    Default Parameters . .  [                      ]          │
│                                                              │
│         ( OK )        ( Cancel )        ( Help )             │
└──────────────────────────────────────────────────────────────┘
```

The text at the top of the box instructs you to *Fill in information for %1 prompt dialog.* The first three *fields* must contain information:

- The first field, called *Window Title*, specifies the title of the dialog box. Sure enough, it contains *File to Edit*.

- The second field, called *Program Information*, specifies the text that appears inside the dialog box at the top. Look back at the File to Edit dialog box as shown above and compare the text at the top of that box with the contents of this field; only the last few words of the text are visible here—*out opening a file, press ENTER*—because the text is much longer than the field. You can see all the text by pressing Tab to move the cursor to this field, pressing Right arrow to clear the highlight, then Left arrow to start scrolling toward the beginning of the text; you can scroll all the way to the beginning of the text by pressing Home.

- The third field, called *Prompt Message*, specifies the text that appears to the left of the field (such as *Program Information* or *Prompt Message* in the dialog box on the screen now). In the File to Edit dialog box, the field is called *File to edit?*, as specified here.

For a quick example of this, you can change the prompt message that the File to Edit dialog box displays. Press Tab again to move to the *Prompt Message* field. Now it reads *File to edit?* Type the following:

```
Type file name:
```

You've changed the words but not the meaning of the prompt message. Now press Enter to complete the change, then choose *Editor* again. Now the File to Edit dialog box shows your prompt message:

Chapter Review

With the Shell features you saw in this chapter, you're ready to start adding your own programs to the Shell, customizing it to the way you use your computer. The main points covered:

- The New command from the File menu lets you add a program item or program group.

- You can create your own Help messages for groups and programs that you add to the program list.

- To delete a program from the program list, highlight it and press Del (deleting a program from a group doesn't delete it from your hard disk).

- You can create dialog boxes that prompt for more information when a program is started from the program list.

CHAPTER

7

RUNNING MORE THAN
ONE PROGRAM
AT A TIME

In previous chapters, you've started programs from the Shell and added programs to the Shell's program list. This final chapter on the Shell shows you a feature that lets you do something you simply can't do any other way using DOS: Start several programs at once, then switch among them with just a keystroke or two. The Shell calls this capability *task swapping*.

If you're continuing from Chapter 6, your screen should show the program and file list areas:

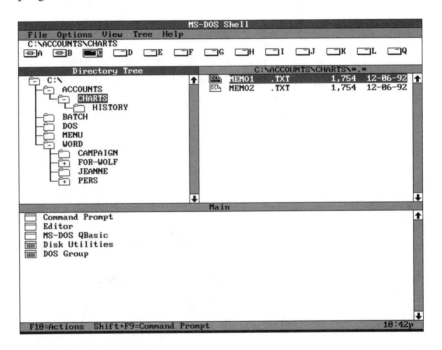

Task swapping isn't always available in the Shell; you turn the capability on and off with the Enable Task Swapper command in the Options menu. Choosing the command alternately turns task swapping on and off; the Shell displays a dot to the left of the Enable Task Swapper command when task swapping is on.

Turn on task swapping now by choosing *Enable Task Swapper* from the Options menu. The Shell divides the program list area at the bottom of the screen, adding an area on the right titled *Active Task List*:

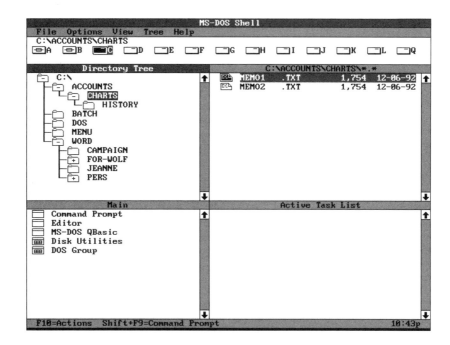

When task swapping is turned on and the program list area is displayed, the active task list lists all the programs you have started. You haven't started any yet, so the list is empty.

Starting More Than One Program

In Chapter 4 you started a program by choosing its name from the program list and by choosing its program file from the file list. When you use task swapping to switch back and forth among programs, you start each program just as you did before; now, however, you can return to the Shell and start another program without quitting the first. If you like, you can return to the Shell and start still another until you have started all your favorite application programs, then switch among them with just a few keystrokes.

To see this, start the DOS Editor by choosing *Editor* from the Main program group. When the Shell prompts you to enter the name of a file to edit, type readme.txt and press Enter. After a few seconds, the opening Editor screen appears. Now press Ctrl+Esc; in a few moments you're back at the Shell screen.

Notice that the active task list now displays *Editor*, the name of the item you chose from the Main program list:

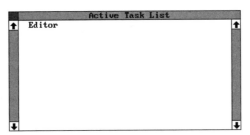

To return to the Editor, choose *Editor* from the active task list (*not* the program list on the left); the screen should look just as it did when you switched away from the Editor a few moments ago. You can switch back and forth between the Editor and the Shell whenever you like by choosing *Editor* from the active task list and pressing Ctrl+Esc to return to the Shell.

Press Ctrl+Esc to return to the Shell.

Building the Active Task List Quickly

That's handy, to be able to use a program and switch back to the Shell whenever you like without ending the program. But the real value of task swapping comes when you start several programs and switch back and forth without ending any of them.

You could start more programs in the same manner you started the Editor, but suppose that you knew you wanted to start several programs; instead of starting each one, then leaving it to return to the Shell and start another, the Shell lets you add a program to the active task list without actually bringing the program to the screen. This is a much quicker way of starting several programs.

To add a program to the active task list without leaving the Shell, you hold down the Shift key while you start the program in the normal fashion. For example, add QBasic to the active task list by holding down Shift and choosing *MS-DOS QBasic* from the Main program group; press Enter in response to the prompt asking for the name of a file to load. Now QBasic appears on the active task list, even though the screen never displayed anything except the Shell.

Your active task list should now contain two entries:

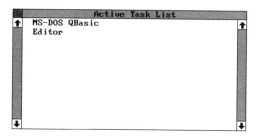

This is the quickest way to add programs to the active task list. If you typically use three or four application programs, the fastest way to start your computer session each day is to start the Shell, then build the active task list, using this technique, before you do anything else.

To switch to a program, you choose it from the active task list. To switch to QBasic, for example, choose it from the active task list. Now here's another way of switching among programs that you might prefer. Hold the Alt key down and press and release the Tab key, but keep holding the Alt key. The screen clears and a title bar at the top reads *MS-DOS Shell*:

But press the Tab key again; now the title bar reads *Editor*. Press Tab again, and the title changes to *MS-DOS QBasic*. Press Tab until the title bar reads *Editor* again, and release the Alt key. You switched directly from QBasic to the Editor.

Pressing Alt+Tab cycles through all the programs in the active task list plus the Shell itself. You can use this technique to switch from the Shell or any active program to any other active program or the Shell. If you're running several programs, you'll probably find this the most convenient way to switch among them.

Return to the Shell either by pressing Ctrl-Esc or by holding down the Alt key and pressing Tab until *MS-DOS Shell* appears at the top of the screen.

Deleting a Program from the Active Task List

When you're through using a program—for the computer session or for the day, not just for the immediate task at hand—you quit the program in the normal fashion, you don't just switch away from it again. Use Alt-Tab to switch to QBasic, press Esc to clear the screen, then choose *Exit* from the File menu to leave QBasic and return to the Shell.

When you return to the Shell, notice that QBasic is no longer in the active task list. If you wanted to switch to QBasic again, you would first have to start it.

You can delete a program from the active task list without ending it in the normal fashion, but you should do this only if some problem with the program prevents you from ending it in the normal fashion. Assuming that the same problem doesn't prevent you from returning to the DOS Shell, you highlight the program in the active task list and press the Del key.

For example, to delete the Editor from the active task list, highlight *Editor* and press Del. The Shell displays this warning message:

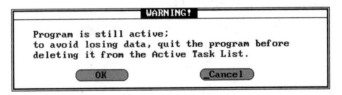

Notice that the cursor is at the beginning of *Cancel*, telling you that pressing Enter heeds the warning and cancels the deletion. Press Enter to cancel.

If you choose *OK* at this message, the Shell ends the program— but not necessarily in an orderly fashion—and deletes it from the active task list; chances are this won't cause a problem, but there is a chance that something could go wrong. To play it safe, if you delete a program from the active task list in this way, you should end the rest of the programs in the active task list in their normal fashion, end the Shell and return to DOS, then restart the Shell.

Defining Your Own Shortcut Key

You've seen a couple of ways to switch back and forth among programs in the active task list: you can press Ctrl+Esc to switch back to the Shell and then choose a different program from the active task list, or you can cycle through the programs you have started by holding down Alt and repeatedly pressing Tab. But there's an even faster way that lets you switch directly to any program in the active task list; it requires just a few moments to set up: a shortcut key.

Many of the menus include shortcut keys for some of their choices: in the File menu, for example, F9 is a shortcut for for View File Contents and Del is a shortcut for Delete; in the Tree menu, + and - are shortcuts for expanding and collapsing a branch. These shortcut keys are shown in the menus to the right of the command name; here's how they look in the Tree menu:

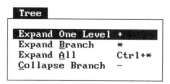

You can define your own shortcut key for any program in the program list; you can't use the shortcut key to start the program, but after you have started it, you can use the shortcut key to switch to the program from any other program.

You assign the shortcut key by highlighting the program name in the program list and choosing *Properties* from the File menu; you enter the shortcut key in the Program Item Properties dialog box. The shortcut key can consist of almost any combination of the Ctrl, Shift, or Alt key plus any other character on the keyboard. You shouldn't use any of the following combinations because DOS itself uses them:

Ctrl+C	Shift+Ctrl+C
Ctrl+I	Shift+Ctrl+I
Ctrl+H	Shift+Ctrl+H
Ctrl+M	Shift+Ctrl+M
Ctrl+[	Shift+Ctrl+[

Ctrl+5   Shift+Ctrl+5 (on the keypad)

Alt+F4

Shift+F5

Follow these steps to assign the shortcut key Ctrl+E to the DOS editor in the Main group:

1. Highlight *Editor* in the Main group.
2. Choose *Properties* from the File menu.
3. Tab down to the *Application Shortcut Key* field.
4. Press *Ctrl+E*, the shortcut key you want to assign.
5. Press Enter twice.

The shortcut key takes effect the next time you start the program. You started the Editor earlier in this chapter, so end it by switching to it, pressing Esc to clear the message, and choosing *Exit* from the File menu. Now add it to the active task list again by holding down Shift and choosing it from the Main program group.

Notice that now the shortcut key is listed after the Editor's name in the active task list:

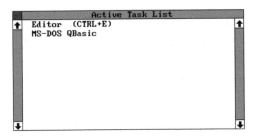

Press Ctrl+E; you should switch to the Editor. You can use the shortcut key to switch directly to a program from the Shell or any other program that you have started.

Chapter Review

That wraps up this chapter—in fact, it concludes your introduction to the DOS Shell. The Shell should now feel more like the comfortable home base referred to in Chapter 1. Clean things up by ending the Editor, QBasic, and any other programs you may have started, and returning to the Shell screen. If you like, you can also delete the directories and files you created; they're all in the branch that starts with the directory named ACCOUNTS.

The most important points covered in this chapter:

- To turn task swapping on or off, choose *Enable Task Swapper* from the Options menu.

- When you start a program with task swapping turned on, you can return to the DOS Shell without ending the program by pressing Ctrl+Esc.

- When you switch out of a program, the program pauses exactly where it is until you return to it.

- To switch from the DOS Shell to any active program, choose the program's name from the active task list.

- To add a program to the active task list without switching to it, hold down the Shift key while starting the program.

- To cycle through the programs in the active task list, hold down the Alt key and repeatedly press Tab; the name of each program (including the Shell itself) appears, in turn, in the title at the top of the screen.

- When you're through using a program, you should end it in the normal manner.

- If a program fails and won't let you end it normally, you can end it by deleting it from the active task list (if the program will let you switch to the Shell); if you do this, however, you should immediately end all other programs, then exit and restart the Shell.

- You can assign a shortcut key to a program; after you have started the program, you can use the shortcut key to switch directly to the program from any other program.

PART II

THE DOS COMMAND LINE

CHAPTER

8

A QUICK TOUR OF DOS FROM THE COMMAND PROMPT

When you operate DOS using the Shell, you choose commands from menus; the only time you have to type something is when the Shell prompts you for a specific item of information, such as the name of a file. If you're not sure exactly how to do something, you can use online help to answer most of your questions. But the Shell isn't the only way to operate DOS. In earlier chapters, you used the DOS Shell to carry out such tasks as copying and deleting files and directories. Most of the tasks you performed can be accomplished just as well, although not as conveniently, by typing at the DOS command prompt. This chapter shows you how to leave the Shell both temporarily and permanently, and it takes you on a quick tour of some common DOS commands.

If the Shell isn't running, DOS waits for your instructions, and the screen is blank except for,

```
C:\_
```

Until version 4 of DOS this was the only way you could operate DOS, unless you bought a Shell program in addition to DOS.

If you're continuing from Chapter 7, however, your screen should look a lot like this:

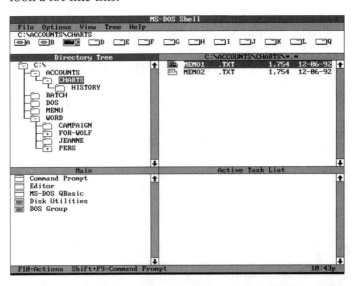

Highlight the DOS directory in the directory tree and then choose *Command Prompt* from the Main program list to leave the Shell temporarily. DOS clears the screen and displays something like this:

```
C:\DOS>
```

This is the DOS *command prompt*, which is how DOS tells you that it's waiting for you to type a command. It doesn't offer any of the clues or aids that the Shell uses to simplify the task of operating DOS, but it isn't difficult to remember and use the few DOS commands that you'll need most of the time.

A command is simply an instruction to DOS. Some commands consist of a single word, while others require additional information, such as the name of a file or directory. To tell DOS to look at what you have typed, you must always press Enter after typing a command. You'll start with a simple command that tells you which version of DOS you're using.

Which Version of DOS Are You Using?

Several versions of DOS have been released since it made its debut in 1981. To keep track of the various versions, the number to the right of the decimal point changes when a minor revision is released, resulting in version numbers such as 3.3 and 4.01. An increase in the number to the left of the decimal point marks a major change, such as versions 5.0 and 6.0.

To see which version of DOS you're using, type the following:

```
ver
```

Press Enter to end the command. DOS responds by displaying its name and version number:

```
MS-DOS Version 6.00
```

The *MS-DOS* indicates that this version of DOS was released by Microsoft. If your system responds with *PC-DOS*, your copy of DOS was released by IBM; if it responds with *Compaq-DOS*, your copy of DOS was released by Compaq.

6.0, of course, is the actual version number.

Working with Directories and Files

In the first part of this book, you used the Shell to create a directory structure and files in those directories. The directories that you saw in the Shell are still on your disk when you're looking at the command prompt, they just aren't as easy to see or use.

The first thing you'll want to know is which directory you're currently working with. The command prompt itself should tell you that; it should read:

```
C:\DOS>
```

If the command prompt doesn't look like this, type the following (don't worry about remembering these commands; you'll work them both a bit later):

```
cd \dos
```

```
prompt $p$g
```

Don't forget to press Enter after each command. Now the command prompt should be *C:\DOS>*.

To see which files are stored in a directory, you use the Dir (for *directory*) command. In its simplest form, Dir displays a list of all files in the current directory and the names of any subdirectories. Try it; type the following (don't forget to press Enter):

```
dir
```

Your screen displays something like this:

```
MSAVIRUS LST     35520 12-06-92     6:00a
MOUSE    INI        28 10-16-93     7:53p
MSAV     HLP     23891 12-06-92     6:00a
MSAVHELP OVL     29828 12-06-92     6:00a
DBLSPACE HLP     35851 12-06-92     6:00a
DBLSPACE INF      1546 12-06-92     6:00a
DBLSPACE SYS       217 12-06-92     6:00a
EMM386   EXE    114782 12-06-92     6:00a
SIZER    EXE      6609 12-06-92     6:00a
MEMMAKER EXE    118398 12-06-92     6:00a
DELTREE  EXE     10271 12-06-92     6:00a
INTERLNK EXE     17133 12-06-92     6:00a
INTERSVR EXE     37266 12-06-92     6:00a
MOVE     EXE     13193 12-06-92     6:00a
MSCDEX   EXE     25399 12-06-92     6:00a
RAMDRIVE SYS      5873 12-06-92     6:00a
SMARTDRV EXE     42073 12-06-92     6:00a
COMMAND  COM     53405 12-06-92     6:00a
DEFAULT  SET      4477 10-16-93     7:24p
DEFAULT  SLT        26 10-16-93     7:24p
MEMMAKER STS      1237 10-16-93     8:59p
       127 file(s)     6044476 bytes
                      15896576 bytes free
```

You probably noticed that the list was too long and scrolled off the top of the screen; all you're seeing is the last screenful. There's a solution for this. Some DOS commands let you add more detail to your instructions in the form of *parameters*—qualifiers that follow the name of the command. One such parameter for the Dir command is /P (for *pause*), which tells DOS to display a screenful of information, then to wait for you to press a key before displaying the next screenful. Type the following:

```
dir /p
```

Now you see the first screenful of output:

```
Volume in drive C is MS-DOS_6
Volume Serial Number is 198C-7A04
Directory of C:\DOS

.                <DIR>      10-16-93  10:58a
..               <DIR>      10-16-93  10:58a
EGA      SYS      4885 12-06-92   6:00a
FORMAT   COM     22070 12-06-92   6:00a
NLSFUNC  EXE      7036 12-06-92   6:00a
COUNTRY  SYS     17066 12-06-92   6:00a
EGA      CPI     58870 12-06-92   6:00a
HIMEM    SYS     13984 12-06-92   6:00a
KEYB     COM     14983 12-06-92   6:00a
KEYBOARD SYS     34694 12-06-92   6:00a
ANSI     SYS      8959 12-06-92   6:00a
ATTRIB   EXE     11165 12-06-92   6:00a
CHOICE   COM      1754 12-06-92   6:00a
CHKDSK   EXE     12058 12-06-92   6:00a
EDIT     COM       413 12-06-92   6:00a
DBLSPACE BIN     65402 12-06-92   6:00a
DEBUG    EXE     15715 12-06-92   6:00a
DOSSWAP  EXE     18756 12-06-92   6:00a
EXPAND   EXE     16129 12-06-92   6:00a
Press any key to continue . . .
```

As you can see, the Dir command output shows you the same information the Shell displayed in the file list. There's no separate directory tree, however; subdirectories are simply identified by *<DIR>* after their name.

Press the space bar (or any other key) to display the remainder of the output. Keep pressing a key until DOS displays the command prompt again.

Getting Help

DOS offers two forms of online help when you're working at the command line—a basic help screen that shows you the parameters of a command and briefly explains their use, and more comprehensive help that describes the purpose as well as the form of a command, gives you hints about how to use it, and shows examples.

To see the basic help screen, you type the name of the command followed by /?. You've seen that the Dir command has several options. Check out the basic help that DOS offers by typing the following:

```
dir /?
```

DOS displays a screenful of information:

```
Displays a list of files and subdirectories in a directory.

DIR [drive:][path][filename] [/P] [/W] [/A[[:]attribs]] [/O[[:]sortord]]
    [/S] [/B] [/L] [/C[H]]

  [drive:][path][filename]    Specifies drive, directory, and/or files to list.
  /P        Pauses after each screenful of information.
  /W        Uses wide list format.
  /A        Displays files with specified attributes.
  attribs   D  Directories     R  Read-only files      H  Hidden files
            S  System files    A  Files ready to archive - Prefix meaning "not"
  /O        List by files in sorted order.
  sortord   N  By name (alphabetic)      S  By size (smallest first)
            E  By extension (alphabetic) D  By date & time (earliest first)
            G  Group directories first   - Prefix to reverse order
            C  By compression ratio (smallest first)
  /S        Displays files in specified directory and all subdirectories.
  /B        Uses bare format (no heading information or summary).
  /L        Uses lowercase.
  /C[H]     Displays file compression ratio; /CH uses host allocation unit size.

Switches may be preset in the DIRCMD environment variable.  Override
preset switches by prefixing any switch with - (hyphen)—for example, /-W.
```

This may look pretty complicated, but you don't need to absorb it all at once. In general, the parameters described here give you the same sort of control over the Dir command output that you had over how the Shell displayed the file list. After the first line, which tells you what the command does, are two lines that show the various parameters you can use with the command. Optional parameters are shown in brackets (notice that all parameters are optional with the Dir command). The remainder of the help screen explains the parameters. You'll use a few of these parameters in a moment.

To get more comprehensive help, you type `help` followed by the name of the command. For example, type the following to see the comprehensive help for the Dir command:

```
help dir
```

This time, DOS displays a screen complete with menu names and cross-references in color:

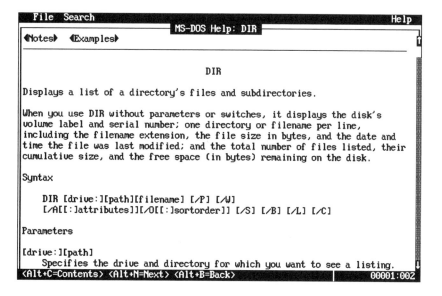

As you can see, the DOS on-line help gives you a fairly complete description of the purpose of the command, plus an explanation of each parameter. The description you're looking at now continues for six more screenfuls; you can scroll through it using either the mouse or cursor control keys (Up Arrow, Down Arrow, PgUp, PgDn, etc.).

But there's more information here about the Dir command. Notice that in the last screen (you can get there quickly by pressing Ctrl-End), under the heading "Related Commands," two command names are enclosed in colored angle brackets: <TREE> and <DBLSPACE>. If you choose either of those terms, DOS displays the opening screen of those command descriptions; these are automatic cross-references.

Notice also that when the opening screen is displayed (you can get there quickly by pressing Ctrl-Home), two words appear below the menu names enclosed in colored triangles: Notes and Examples. Choosing either of these displays still more information about the use of the Dir command. To check out this additional information, choose Examples (either click it with the mouse or tab to it and press Enter); now DOS shows you some examples of how to type the Dir command:

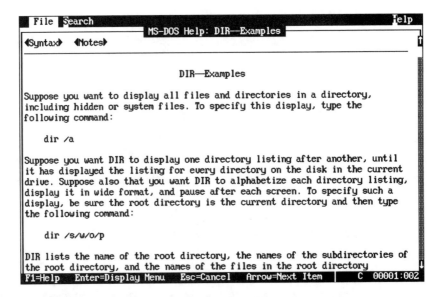

DOS shows you several examples of how to use the command. Notice that the two terms below the menu names are now Syntax and Notes; you're looking at the Examples, so Syntax is offered as a choice to take you back to the description of the form of the command and the parameters.

If you want to see the on-line help information for another command that isn't cross-referenced, you can display the list of all help topics by pressing Alt-C (the bottom line of the screen reminds you of this). Press Alt-C; DOS displays the contents list of all help topics:

```
 File  Search                                                    Help
┌─────────────────────── MS-DOS Help: Command Reference ──────────────────────┐
│                                                                             ▓│
│ Use the scroll bars to see more commands. Or, press the PAGE DOWN key. For  ▓│
│ more information about using MS-DOS Help, choose How to Use MS-DOS Help      ▓│
│ from the Help menu, or press F1. To exit MS-DOS Help, press ALT, F, X.      ▓│
│                                                                             ▓│
│ <ANSI.SYS>               <Fastopen>               <Net Start>               │
│ <Append>                 <Fc>                      <Net Stop>                │
│ <Attrib>                 <Fcbs>                     <Net Time>               │
│ <Batch commands>         <Fdisk>                    <Net Use>                │
│ <Break>                  <Files>                    <Net Ver>                │
│ <Buffers>                <Find>                     <Net View>               │
│ <Call>                   <For>                      <Nlsfunc>                │
│ <Cd>                     <Format>                   <Numlock>                │
│ <Chcp>                   <Goto>                     <Path>                   │
│ <Chdir>                  <Graphics>                 <Pause>                  │
│ <Chkdsk>                 <Help>                     <Power>                  │
│ <CHKSTATE.SYS>           <HIMEM.SYS>                <POWER.EXE>              │
│ <Choice>                 <If>                       <Print>                  │
│ <Cls>                    <Include>                  <Prompt>                 │
│ <Command>                <Install>                  <Qbasic>                 │
│ <CONFIG.SYS commands>    <Interlnk>                 <RAMDRIVE.SYS>           │
│ <Copy>                   <INTERLNK.EXE>             <Rd>                    ▓│
├─────────────────────────────────────────────────────────────────────────────┤
│ <Alt+C=Contents> <Alt+N=Next> <Alt+B=Back>              │ C  00006:002       │
└─────────────────────────────────────────────────────────────────────────────┘
```

Each topic is enclosed in colored angle brackets, meaning that you can jump directly to the help information for any topic just by choosing its entry on the contents screen. You can scroll through the list of topics just as you scroll through any other list using the mouse or cursor control keys. This contents list is especially helpful when you know that there is a command to do what you want, but you can't remember its name. You can display the contents screen directly from the command prompt by typing help by itself.

Online help offers you a description of the form and use of every DOS command, plus some of the associated programs and files included with DOS. It's a quick way to refresh your memory about a command you haven't used in a while, or to learn how to use a command you haven't yet tried. You'll probably find that you seldom need to look at the manual or any other book for basic operating information about DOS when online help is just a few keystrokes away.

To leave online help, choose Exit from the File menu just as you would from the Shell, and DOS returns to the command prompt.

Controlling the Order of File Names

One of the ways you changed the way the Shell displays the file list was to tell it to display just the files whose name was DOSSHELL. You can do the same with the Dir command by specifying a file name; notice that in the second line of the help screen the third parameter is [filename]. Type the following:

```
dir dosshell.*
```

This Dir command output shows only six files:

```
 Volume in drive C is MS-DOS_6
 Volume Serial Number is 198C-7A04
 Directory of C:\DOS

DOSSHELL INI      17648 10-16-93   11:11p
DOSSHELL VID       9462 12-06-92    6:00a
DOSSHELL COM       4620 12-06-92    6:00a
DOSSHELL GRB       4421 12-06-92    6:00a
DOSSHELL EXE     236378 12-06-92    6:00a
DOSSHELL HLP     161323 12-06-92    6:00a
        6 file(s)      433852 bytes
                    16799744 bytes free
```

The Shell normally displays the file list in alphabetic order, but the Dir command shows them in the order in which they're stored on the disk. The /O (for *order*) parameter lets you specify the order in which the files should be listed. You follow the O with N for name, E for extension, S for size, or D for date and time. You can reverse any of these by preceding the letter with a minus sign. (To see how DOS tells you this, type help dir again and look about halfway down the screen for *O* with *sortorder* under it.)

To tell the Dir command to display the files in alphabetic order, you use the /O parameter, specifying N for file name and a hyphen to reverse the order. Type the following (you'll use the /P parameter, too, so you can read all of the output):

```
dir /o-n /p
```

Note that you type a slash (/) before each parameter that follows the command. DOS displays the file names, starting with XCOPY .EXE, the last name in the list:

```
Volume in drive C is MS-DOS_6
Volume Serial Number is 198C-7A04
Directory of C:\DOS

XCOPY    EXE    15820 12-06-92    6:00a
WNTOOLS  GRP     2205 10-16-93    8:26p
VSAFE    COM    62304 12-06-92    6:00a
VFINTD   386     5295 12-06-92    6:00a
UNFORMAT COM    12738 12-06-92    6:00a
UNDELETE EXE    26292 12-06-92    6:00a
TREE     COM     6898 12-06-92    6:00a
SYS      COM     9364 12-06-92    6:00a
SUBST    EXE    18478 12-06-92    6:00a
SORT     EXE     6922 12-06-92    6:00a
SMARTMON EXE    28672 12-06-92    6:00a
SMARTMON HLP    10727 12-06-92    6:00a
SMARTDRV EXE    42073 12-06-92    6:00a
SIZER    EXE     6609 12-06-92    6:00a
SHARE    EXE    10912 12-06-92    6:00a
SETVER   EXE    12015 10-16-93    3:16p
RESTORE  EXE    38294 12-06-92    6:00a
REPLACE  EXE    20226 12-06-92    6:00a
README   TXT    42618 12-06-92    6:00a
Press any key to continue . . .
```

If you didn't put the hyphen before the N, DOS would display the file names in alphabetic order, and the list would begin with EGA.SYS, just as it did in the Shell.

Try one last variation on the Dir command. The /W (for *wide*) parameter tells DOS to display just the names of the files in five columns across the screen. This fits a lot more files in the display, but gives you less information about them. Type the following:

```
dir /w
```

Even though this displays the names of 95 files, all the DOS files still won't fit in one screen:

```
SYS.COM        DOSSHELL.INI   UNFORMAT.COM   XCOPY.EXE      DOSSHELL.VID
MOUSE.INI      DOSSHELL.COM   DOSSHELL.GRB   DEFRAG.EXE     DEFRAG.HLP
MOUSE.COM      QBASIC.HLP     SMARTMON.EXE   SMARTMON.HLP   DISPLAY.SYS
APPEND.EXE     APPNOTES.TXT   DELOLDOS.EXE   DISKCOMP.COM   DISKCOPY.COM
DRIVER.SYS     DOSSHELL.EXE   DOSSHELL.HLP   DOSHELP.EXE    DOSHELP.HLP
DOSKEY.COM     EDIT.HLP       FC.EXE         FIND.EXE       GRAPHICS.COM
GRAPHICS.PRO   HELP.HLP       MWBACKUP.EXE   MWBACKUP.HLP   HELP.COM
LABEL.EXE      LOADFIX.COM    SETVER.EXE     SORT.EXE       FASTOPEN.EXE
MODE.COM       PRINT.EXE      POWER.EXE      README.TXT     REPLACE.EXE
SHARE.EXE      SUBST.EXE      TREE.COM       VFINTD.386     MWBACKF.DLL
MWBACKR.DLL    MSBACKUP.EXE   MSBACKUP.OVL   MSBACKFB.OVL   MSBACKFR.OVL
MSBACKDB.OVL   MSBACKDR.OVL   MSBCONFG.OVL   MSBACKUP.HLP   MSBCONFG.HLP
CHKSTATE.SYS   MEMMAKER.HLP   MEMMAKER.INF   UNDELETE.EXE   MWUNDEL.EXE
MWUNDEL.HLP    WNTOOLS.GRP    MWGRAFIC.DLL   MSTOOLS.DLL    MWAVDOSL.DLL
MWAVDRVL.DLL   MWAVDLG.DLL    MWAVSCAN.DLL   MWAV.EXE       MWAVABSI.DLL
MWAV.HLP       MWAVSOS.DLL    MWAVMGR.DLL    MWAVTSR.EXE    VSAFE.COM
MSAV.EXE       DBLSPACE.EXE   MSAVIRUS.LST   MSAV.HLP       MSAVHELP.OVL
DBLSPACE.HLP   DBLSPACE.INF   DBLSPACE.SYS   EMM386.EXE     SIZER.EXE
MEMMAKER.EXE   DELTREE.EXE    INTERLNK.EXE   INTERSVR.EXE   MOVE.EXE
MSCDEX.EXE     RAMDRIVE.SYS   SMARTDRV.EXE   COMMAND.COM    DEFAULT.SET
DEFAULT.SLT    MEMMAKER.STS
       127 file(s)   6044476 bytes
                16799744 bytes free
```

This display is a good way to check which files are in a directory that contains a large number of files. You can use the /P and the /W parameters together, if necessary, to check directories with a particularly large number of files, like the DOS directory. Depending on what you're looking for, it may be more convenient to use the /O option to control the order in which the files are displayed, or even wildcard characters to limit the number of files displayed. The Dir command offers all the flexibility you need to keep track of your files.

Clearing the Screen of Clutter

As you enter commands at the DOS prompt, the screen fills with the commands you type and DOS's responses, pushing the prompt down until it reaches the bottom of the screen. As more text is displayed, old text scrolls up and off the top of the screen. If you no longer need what's on the screen, you can clean things up with the CLS (Clear Screen) command. Try it; type the following:

```
cls
```

Now the screen shows only the command prompt.

Changing the Current Directory

In the Shell you highlighted a directory in the directory tree to make it the current directory. The CD (for *Change Directory*) command does this at the command prompt. For example, to make the root directory the current directory, type the following (remember, the name of the root directory is \, the backslash symbol):

```
cd \
```

The command prompt should show that the root directory is now the current directory:

```
C:\>
```

See what files the Dir command shows you; type the following:

```
dir /p
```

The third line of the output should tell you that you're looking at the names of the files in C:\.

Viewing a File

You viewed a file in the Shell by choosing *View* from the File menu. The DOS command that comes the closest to this is Type. The current directory should be the root; type the following to display the file named AUTOEXEC.BAT:

```
type autoexec.bat
```

DOS should show you something like this:

```
@echo off
path=c:\dos;c:\windows;c:\batch;c:\word;c:\tt
break on
set temp=c:\temp
set comspec=c:\dos\command.com
LH /L:1,56928 c:\dos\mouse.com
LH /L:1,6400 c:\dos\doskey
LH /L:0;1,42480 /S C:\DOS\SMARTDRV.EXE
```

AUTOEXEC.BAT is a file of commands that DOS carries out each time you start or restart your system. Your output will be different, but some of the commands should be similar.

It isn't nearly as convenient to view a file using the Type command as it is in the Shell, especially if the file is longer than a screenful, because the text scrolls past too quickly to read. In the Shell, you can scroll back and forth in a long file. You can, if you wish, stop the scrolling by pressing the Pause key and resume scrolling by pressing any other key, but it's still pretty hard to get a good look at a file.

Returning to the Shell

You haven't really ended the Shell, you just left it suspended while you worked at the DOS command prompt. The DOS Exit command returns you to the Shell (or any other program that lets you temporarily exit to the DOS command prompt). To return to the Shell, type the following:

```
exit
```

You're right back where you were; nothing has changed because the Shell hasn't been running since you left.

Temporarily leaving the Shell, as you did earlier, isn't the only way to work at the command prompt; you can permanently end the Shell by choosing *Exit* from the File menu. Sometimes this may be preferable because it makes more memory available at the command prompt. Leave the Shell permanently now by choosing *Exit* from the File menu. Once again, DOS displays the command prompt.

Chapter Review

This chapter introduced the basic techniques of controlling DOS by typing commands at the command prompt. The most important points covered in this chapter:

- All the file management tasks you performed using the Shell can also be performed using DOS commands.

- The Ver command displays the version of DOS running on your computer.

- The CLS (Clear Screen) command removes everything from the screen except the DOS prompt.

- To get help for a particular command, type the name of the command followed by /?.

- DOS includes an on-line help facility. To see an index of the help topics, type `help`.

- Some commands include additional qualifiers, called parameters. The help information for a command shows optional parameters enclosed in square brackets ([ ]).

- The Dir command displays a list of file names, sizes, dates, and times in the current directory; or Dir and a path displays information about files in another directory.

- The /O (*order*) parameter of the Dir command controls the order in which the file names are listed. They can be ordered by name, extension, size, or date, either from first to last or last to first.

- The /P (*pause*) parameter of the Dir command displays the file list one screen at a time; the /W parameter creates a multi-column display.

- The CD (Change Directory) command lets you specify the current directory.

- The Type command displays the contents of a file. If the file is longer than a screenful, you can pause the display by pressing the Pause key; pressing any key resumes the display.

CHAPTER

9

WORKING WITH THE DOS UTILITIES

In addition to the Shell and the commands—several of which you'll use in the next few chapters—DOS includes several utility programs that offer capabilities that you used to be able to get only by buying separate programs. These utility programs look something like the Shell, in that they display menus and prompts and let you use either the keyboard or the mouse to operate them.

The four DOS utility programs include:

- DBLSPACE which, by compressing files, in effect doubles the capacity of your hard disk.
- MSBACKUP, which lets you make backup copies of your hard disk files quickly and easily.
- DEFRAG, which packs files more closely on your hard disk to improve performance.
- MSAV, which checks your disks for virus programs.

Although a complete description of these programs is beyond the scope of a brief introductory book like this one, you'll find that these programs are so easy to use—and include such thorough on-line help —that you won't need much more practice than this chapter offers.

Doubling the Size of Your Hard Disk

You may not have had time yet to experience one of the more frustrating qualities of a hard disk: Files somehow proliferate to fill all available disk space in far less time than originally thought possible. Until recently, when you started running out of disk space—and you will run out of disk space, it's just a question of how soon—your only choices were to savagely prune unused or less important files, or buy another hard disk. But now DOS offers a third alternative: The DBLSPACE program, which doubles the capacity of your hard disk without costing you another cent for hardware or software.

DBLSPACE works this bit of apparent magic by compressing all the files on your hard disk, then expanding them as you use them and compressing them again when storing revised versions. All this compressing and expanding is done without any attention from you, and without causing any significant slowdown in performance.

If you haven't yet installed DBLSPACE to double your disk space, you should do it now. Using DBLSPACE is simplicity itself: just type dblspace. The opening screen gives you the choice of continuing, getting help, or leaving:

```
┌─────────────────────────────────────────────────────────────────┐
│ Microsoft DoubleSpace Setup                                       │
│ ══════════════════════════                                        │
│                                                                   │
│        Welcome to DoubleSpace Setup.                              │
│                                                                   │
│        The Setup program for DoubleSpace frees space on your hard │
│        disk by compressing the existing files on the disk. Setup  │
│        also loads DBLSPACE.BIN, the portion of MS-DOS that provides│
│        access to DoubleSpace compressed drives. DBLSPACE.BIN      │
│        requires about 40K of memory.                              │
│                                                                   │
│          o To set up DoubleSpace now, press ENTER.                │
│                                                                   │
│          o To learn more about DoubleSpace Setup, press F1.       │
│                                                                   │
│          o To quit Setup without installing DoubleSpace, press F3.│
│                                                                   │
│                                                                   │
│                                                                   │
│                                                                   │
│                                                                   │
│ ENTER=Continue  F1=Help  F3=Exit                                  │
└─────────────────────────────────────────────────────────────────┘
```

Press Enter to choose Continue. Next, DBLSPACE gives you a choice between what it calls *Express Setup*, where it makes most of the decisions, and *Custom Setup*, which asks you to make the decisions. Unless you know that you'll want to control the process, press Enter to choose Express Setup.

Now DBLSPACE displays a screen that estimates how long it will take to compress your hard disk and gives you a last chance to stop before the compression process begins:

```
┌─────────────────────────────────────────────────────────────────┐
│ Microsoft DoubleSpace Setup                                       │
│ ══════════════════════════                                        │
│                                                                   │
│        DoubleSpace is ready to compress drive C. This will take 10│
│        minutes.                                                   │
│                                                                   │
│        During this process, DoubleSpace will restart your computer│
│        to load DBLSPACE.BIN, the portion of MS-DOS that provides  │
│        access to DoubleSpace compressed drives.                   │
│                                                                   │
│                                                                   │
│        To compress this drive, press C.                           │
│        To return to the previous screen, press ESC.               │
│                                                                   │
│                                                                   │
│                                                                   │
│                                                                   │
│                                                                   │
│                                                                   │
│ C=Continue  F1=Help  F3=Exit  ESC=Previous screen                 │
└─────────────────────────────────────────────────────────────────┘
```

Press C to start compressing. It will show you how much available space there now is on your hard disk; you'll be pleasantly surprised. Press Enter to restart your system to load the part of DBLSPACE that remains in memory whenever your system is running.

After you have installed DBLSPACE, you can use your system just as you did before. There's no difference in how you manage your files, and usually no perceptible difference in system performance, even though DBLSPACE is expanding files when you use them and compressing them when they're stored on the disk. Although DBL-SPACE offers a few more options, this is all you really need to know (and all you need to do) to enjoy the benefits of a hard disk twice its original size.

Making Backup Copies of Your Hard Disk Files

Hard disks are remarkably durable, but sometimes they do fail, causing bad things to happen to your files. More bad things happen to files, unfortunately due to pilot error: Someday, certainly, you will tell DOS to delete a file—or even a directory full of files—that you really need. As you'll see in a future chapter, you can recover deleted files with the Undelete command, but only if you haven't stored more files on the disk. Your chance of recovering a deleted file diminishes drastically if you continue using the system before attempting to recover it.

The answer is to make backup copies of your files—at least the ones you work with, the data files such as word processor documents or spreadsheets—from the hard disk to floppy disks. The MSBACK-UP program expedites this job, letting you choose which files to back up from a list much like the Shell's File List and making the backup copies much faster than you could do it using the Copy or Xcopy commands. The first time you use MSBACKUP you will need one or two floppy disks that fit the drive you will be using. Make sure they do not contain any files you need as MSBACKUP will delete any files which are on the disk.

To start MSBACKUP, type `msbackup`. If this is the first time the program has been run on your system, you'll see a dialog box that tells you *Backup requires configuration for this computer* and offers just two choices: *Start configuration* and *Quit*:

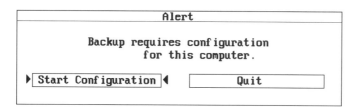

MSBACKUP has extensive on-line help; you'll use it, in fact, to guide yourself through trying out the program. To see what this screen means, for example, press F1 (the key you'll always use to get on-line help):

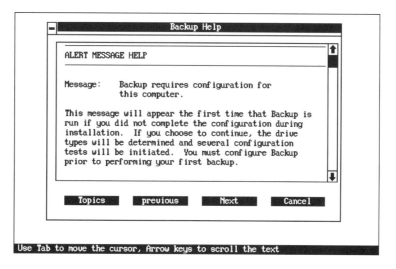

This screen explains that MSBACKUP has to check what type of disk drives you have and learn a few other things about your system before it can start backing up files. Before you start the configuration process, take a few minutes to check out the MSBACKUP on-line help. Notice that there is a menu with four choices—*Topics*, *Previous*, *Next*, and *Cancel*—at the bottom of the dialog box, and the bottom line of the screen tells you how to navigate. Choose *Topics* (just as in the Shell, either highlight it with the Tab key and press Enter or click on it with the mouse) and MSBACKUP displays the list of its on-line help topics. Scroll down a few lines to see the first few topics:

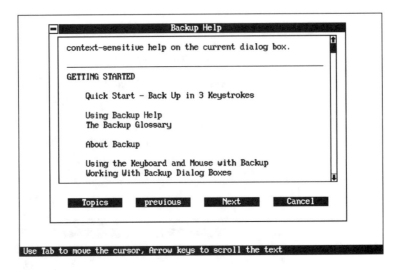

At this point you might want to spend a bit of time reading some of the help topics to learn how MSBACKUP does its job. A good place to start might be the second topic, *Using Backup Help*, which shows you how to find just what you're looking for and how to move back and forth in the help information. You can scroll through the list of help topics with the cursor control keys and select topics with the Tab key or mouse (use Shift-Tab to move the highlight up the list instead of down the list).

Remember, you can always call on on-line help for more information. For now, it's time to go on with MSBACKUP. Press Esc (more than once, if necessary) to clear the help screen and return to the opening display. If this is the first time MSBACKUP has run, you're being offered the choice of *Start configuration* or *Quit* (if your screen offers more choices, like the next screen display shown, skim the next couple of paragraphs until the description matches your screen).

Configuration simply means that MSBACKUP wants to find out what sort of floppy disk drives you have, how big your hard disk is, and a few other items of information it uses to prepare itself. The process is basically an automated run-through of a sample backup session using your DOS files and a couple of floppy disks that fit the drive you'll be using to back up your files. When you've got the disks at hand—make sure they don't contain any files you need—press Enter to start configuration.

Now watch the screen as MSBACKUP behaves as if someone were backing up some files. The program pauses several times to ask you some questions; you also put disks in and out when instructed. Press Enter to accept the suggested answer until the process ends. Now MSBACKUP is ready to run; it displays the main menu screen:

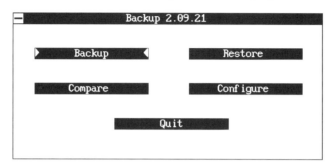

To back up files, choose *Back up*. Now MSBACKUP displays the Backup screen, which lets you choose the hard disk from which to back up files, the floppy disk drive that contains the backup disks, the files to back up, and when to start the process. Drive C should be displayed as the hard disk and drive A displayed as the floppy disk:

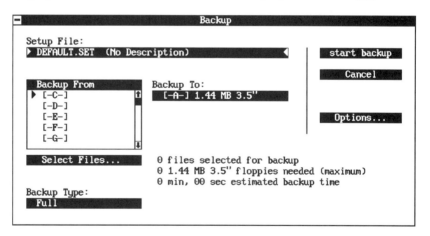

Choose *Select Files . . .* to see the file from which you choose the files to back up, and you'll see a screen much like the DOS Shell: disk drive letters across the top of the screen, directory tree on the left, list of files on the right, and some menu choices across the bottom. Choose the DOS directory in the directory tree, and you should see the beginning of the list of DOS files:

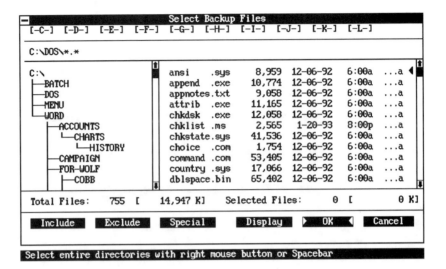

This is where you decide which files to back up. Generally speaking, all you really need worry about are the files that you change, such as word processor documents, spreadsheets, and database files. Just choose the proper directory in the directory tree, then choose the files either by highlighting them with the cursor control keys and pressing the space bar or clicking them with the right mouse button.

When you have chosen the files, press Esc to return to the Backup screen, then choose *Start Backup*. MSBACKUP prompts you to make sure the proper disk is in drive A, then begins the process. Restoring files follows essentially the same procedure; remember, you can use on-line help to guide you through any procedures you aren't familiar with or that you haven't used in a while.

To leave MSBACKUP, press Esc until the main menu is on the screen and *Quit* is highlighted, then press Enter. Because MSBACKUP simplifies the process of backing up files, it should encourage you to back up your files regularly. Even though it takes a bit of time and even though hard disk drives seldom fail, just one failure could cost you far more time than you would ever spend backing up your files.

Packing Files More Tightly on Your Hard Disk

Using files is almost synonymous with using your computer. No matter what sort of programs you use, you'll create new files, change existing files, and delete files you don't need any more. DOS tries to store a file in a single location on a disk, but all this activity tends to fragment the space, chopping it up into smaller and smaller pieces. As a result, DOS often must store a file—particularly a large file—in several small locations and keep track of how the parts must be strung together to recreate the entire file. A file fragmented like this is more cumbersome for programs to use and causes your system to slow down a bit.

The DOS program DEFRAG (for *Defragment*) packs all the files into contiguous locations. Depending on what sort of programs and how many files you use, this can speed up your system from barely noticeable to a significant difference.

To start DEFRAG, type defrag; the program displays its opening screen, which most likely offers to optimize drive C, your hard disk:

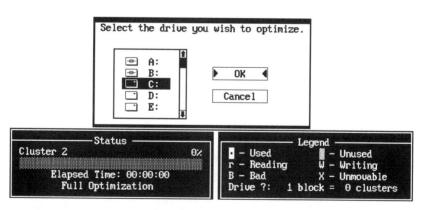

Press Enter (or click on OK to accept the suggestion, and DE-FRAG displays a map of how space is used on the disk and a dialog box that suggests the sort of optimization your disk needs:

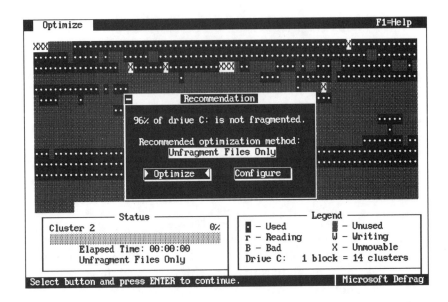

Unless you have a very large hard disk that is badly fragmented, the process takes just a few minutes, so highlight *Optimize* and press Enter to start. As DEFRAG moves files around to pack them into contiguous spaces, you can watch the progress on the disk map; the legend for the map is in the lower right corner.

DEFRAG notifies you when it finishes optimizing (or *condensing*, as the message says). You have exercised the primary functions of DEFRAG, and your disk should operate more efficiently now. For more information about other features of DEFRAG, press Enter to clear the Finished condensing message; DEFRAG displays a dialog box that gives you the choice of choosing another drive to optimize, configuring the program, or leaving DEFRAG. Notice that in the upper right corner it tells you that you can press F1 to get help. Press F1, and DEFRAG displays its opening Help screen. As you can see, the on-line help not only tells you how to use DEFRAG, it even tells you how to use help.

If you want more information now, follow the instructions and use the help feature to find the information you want. When you're ready to leave DEFRAG, press Esc to leave the help feature, then choose *Exit DEFRAG* from the dialog box (or, if the dialog box is gone, choose *Exit* from the Optimize menu just as you chose Exit from the File menu in the Shell).

Protecting Yourself Against Virus Programs

A virus program is designed to attach itself to or bury itself within a file on a floppy disk or your hard disk, thereby escaping casual detection. At some point, determined by the date or how many times you have used your system since the virus program found its way in, the virus will do something irritating—such as display messages or otherwise interfere with normal system operation—or something destructive, such as damaging or deleting files on your hard disk. In some cases, a virus can reformat your hard disk, wiping out all your programs and data.

Viruses aren't widespread. The chance that you'll encounter one is rare, especially if you don't download programs from computer bulletin boards or swap programs on unlabeled disks. But the consequences are serious enough to merit some defensive measures. DOS includes an anti-virus program called MSAV (for *Microsoft Anti-Virus*) that is simple to use and quickly checks all the files on your hard disk. To start MSAV, type msav; it displays its opening screen:

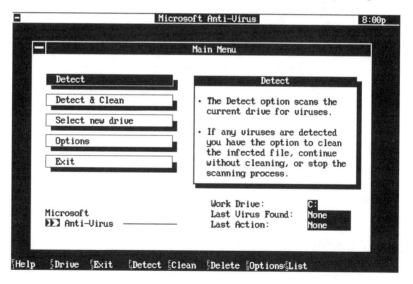

Although the screen displays a menu of several choices, the action you'll most frequently want to take is the highlighted first choice, *Detect*, which searches for any oddities in your files that would indicate that a virus might be present, and then gives you a choice of actions. It takes only a few minutes to check a disk, so press Enter to accept the highlighted choice.

Now MSAV changes the screen to show you its progress as it checks each file on your hard disk. If MSAV should find something amiss, it displays the name of the file and the circumstances it finds curious, then gives you the option of deleting the file or continuing without taking any action. If you're not sure what the file is or where the original is, don't delete it, but ask a more experienced user to look at the situation.

When MSAV finishes, it displays a summary of what it found:

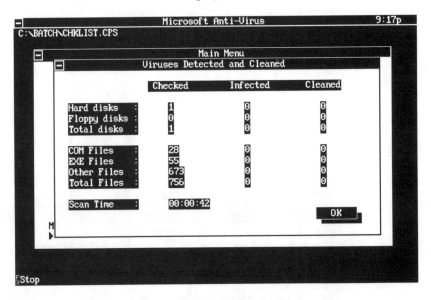

When you press Enter to clear this screen, MSAV returns you to the original menu screen, shown earlier. Like the other DOS utility programs, MSAV includes on-line help that you start by pressing F1. When you're ready to leave MSAV, press Esc and Enter.

Chapter Review

This chapter gave you a quick look at four DOS utility programs. The most important points covered in this chapter:

- DBLSPACE, MSBACKUP, DEFRAG, and MSAV are DOS utilities that let you use menus and a mouse to control them.

- All four utilities include online help to guide you through their operation.

- DBLSPACE can increase the capacity of your hard disk by up to 100 percent without changing the way you use your system or affecting its performance.

- MSBACKUP makes it quick and easy to back up files from your hard disk to floppy disks.

- DEFRAG rearranges the files on your hard disk to make sure that each file is stored in a contiguous area, which can speed up disk operations.

- MSAV checks your system for virus programs and can guard continuously against virus programs.

- DOS also includes versions of MSBACKUP and MSAV that run under Windows.

CHAPTER

10

WORKING WITH DISKETTES

Hard disks are the most labor-saving devices in the development of personal computers. True, speedy microprocessors and larger memories let systems run more quickly, but large, fast hard disks not only save us the tedium of frequently exchanging diskettes, they actually make it possible to develop the comprehensive, versatile application programs used on today's computers.

However, despite the speed and convenience of a hard disk, the slower, smaller diskette still plays a major role in using a computer. Virtually every program you install on your computer comes on diskettes; whenever you share your work with someone or back up your hard disk, chances are that you'll use a diskette.

In this chapter you'll prepare a diskette for use in your computer with the Format command, then see how the Unformat command lets you recover from a potentially costly mistake. You'll also create a system diskette, which you can use to start your computer if something should happen to the hard disk, and you'll copy an entire diskette with one command.

For the examples in this chapter, you'll need two diskettes, either new ones or diskettes that contain files you no longer need.

Varieties of Diskettes

Diskettes come in two types: 3.5-inch diskettes are enclosed in a rigid plastic shell; 5.25-inch diskettes come in a flexible plastic case (which is why diskettes are also called floppy disks). Your computer could have either type of diskette drive or, as is becoming increasingly common, both. Within these two types are several variations in storage capacity.

Disk storage capacity is measured in bytes; one byte is the amount of storage necessary to store a single character (letter, number, or punctuation mark). Just as highway distances are expressed in kilometers (1,000 meters) rather than meters, storage capacity is expressed in either kilobytes (slightly more than 1,000 bytes, abbreviated K) or megabytes (slightly more than 1,000,000 bytes, abbreviated M).

The capacity of a diskette depends on both the type of diskette and the type of diskette drive in which it's used. A 5.25-inch diskette can store either 360K or 1.2M; a 3.5-inch diskette can store either

720K (kilobytes), 1.44M (megabytes), or 2.88M. To put this in more familiar terms, a page of single-spaced typewritten text contains about 3,000 characters. So, depending on its capacity, a diskette can hold enough text to fill 120 to 960 average typewritten pages; the most commonly used diskettes (1.2M and 1.44M) hold the equivalent of 400 to 480 typewritten pages.

In general, newer machines offer the higher diskette storage capacities in each type. Most computers manufactured since 1987 have either 1.2M or 1.44M diskette drives.

Preparing a Diskette for Use

Before you can store any files on a new diskette, you must prepare it by putting it in the diskette drive and typing the Format command. This process is called *formatting* the disk.

The simplest form of the Format command requires just the command name and the letter of the diskette drive. Like many other commands, Format includes parameters that let you specify more precisely what you want. Because of the many different types of diskettes used since the PC was first released in 1981, the Format command has many parameters. In most cases, however, the only parameter you'll need is the drive letter.

> **Note**
>
> The Format command can also prepare a hard disk. Because formatting erases all files on a disk, you *really* don't want to inadvertently format your hard disk. Because of the potential for calamity, DOS insists that you specify the drive letter with the Format command; if you specify the drive letter of your hard disk, DOS displays an ominous warning message and requires you to confirm that you indeed want to format your hard disk before continuing.

You must format a new diskette before you can use it, but DOS will format any diskette you put in the drive. If you do format a diskette that has been previously formatted and used to store files, the formatting process erases any files that are stored on the diskette. For this reason, be sure that you're formatting the correct diskette. (DOS 5 does allow you to recover files erased by formatting—in some cases. We'll try this shortly.)

Protecting a Diskette against Change

To avoid inadvertently changing or deleting files, both types of diskettes include a mechanism for preventing any changes to the contents of the diskette. This feature is called *write protection*. A write-protected diskette can't be changed; all you can do is read files from it (you can't even store a new file on it). Because formatting requires writing on the diskette, DOS can't format a write-protected diskette.

Write-protecting either size diskette involves controlling the passage of light through a hole or notch in the diskette case. Look at the diskette you're going to format and compare it to the following illustration:

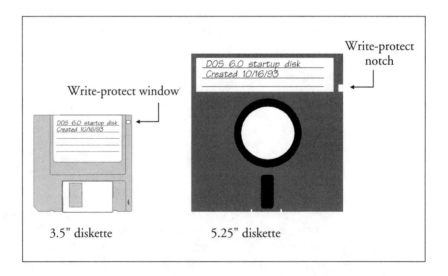

Write-protect notch

Write-protect window

DOS 6.0 startup disk
Created 10/16/93

DOS 6.0 startup disk
Created 10/16/93

3.5" diskette   5.25" diskette

A 3.5-inch diskette has a write-protect hole in the corner to the right of the label, as shown in the illustration. On the back of the disk (the side away from the label) is a small cover that can be slid over the hole. If the hole is covered, the disk can be changed; if the hole isn't covered, the disk is write-protected. In the other corner of the diskette, there may also be a hole that doesn't have a sliding cover; this hole identifies the diskette as high density—1.44M (megabytes) instead of 720K (kilobytes).

A 5.25-inch disk has a notch cut out of the edge to the right of the label, as shown in the illustration, but reverses the rule above: If the notch is uncovered, the disk can be changed; if the notch is covered with a piece of tape, the disk is write-protected.

A small light inside the diskette drive just above the write-protect notch or hole, working in concert with a light-sensitive device below the hole, lets the diskette drive determine whether the diskette is write-protected. So, check the appropriate opening on your diskette to make sure that it isn't write-protected, and put it in the drive.

Formatting a Diskette Unconditionally

The Format command offers several different ways to format a diskette. You'll try a couple of them in this chapter. The first of these is called an *unconditional* format; this process erases everything on the disk and cannot be reversed.

To format the diskette unconditionally, put it in drive A and type the following (end the command by pressing Enter):

```
format a: /u
```

DOS responds by prompting you to put the diskette in the drive you specified and press Enter:

```
Insert new diskette for drive A:
and press ENTER when ready...
```

The diskette is already in the drive, so press Enter again. DOS responds by telling you the storage capacity it is formatting and how much of the disk it has formatted:

```
Formatting 1.44M
   1 percent completed.
```

Depending on the size diskette you're using, the first message on your screen might be different. DOS continues to update the percentage complete until the disk is formatted (this will take a couple of minutes), then replaces the line with the message *Format complete* and prompts you to enter a name for the diskette (DOS calls this name the *volume label*):

```
Volume label (11 characters, ENTER for none)?
```

Later on, when you use the Dir command to see the contents of this diskette, DOS will include any name you specify. A name isn't required but can be useful, so type fred and press Enter. Now DOS shows you the diskette's vital statistics:

```
1457664 bytes total disk space
1457664 bytes available on disk
    512 bytes in each allocation unit.
   2847 allocation units available on disk.

Volume Serial Number is 1861-674C

Format another (Y/N)?
```

This shows the report for a 3.5-inch high-density diskette, which can store 1.44M. If your diskettes are a different size, of course, your report will include different numbers. If your diskette includes any bad sectors, they also will be included in the report. The *Volume Serial Number* (*1861-674C* in the example) is an identifying number that DOS itself randomly assigns to the diskette; yours will be different. (The name you gave the disk—*FRED*—is the volume label, not the volume serial number.)

DOS ends this dialog by asking you if you'd like to format another diskette. It does this to save you the trouble of typing the Format command again when you're formatting several diskettes at once. Formatting several diskettes isn't that unusual; people often format an entire box of diskettes after they buy it, so that all the diskettes will be ready to use.

You're not going to format another diskette just yet, so press N and Enter. DOS displays the command prompt and waits for you to type another command.

Copying Files to a Diskette

In the Shell, you made a disk drive the current drive by highlighting its drive letter at the top of the screen. At the command prompt, you make a disk drive the current drive by typing its drive letter followed by a colon, then pressing Enter. Type the following to make drive A the current drive:

```
a:
```

The command prompt changes to *A:\>*, confirming that drive A is the current drive. From now on, DOS assumes that any command you enter should apply to the disk in drive A and not to drive C as it did before (unless you include a drive letter in the command). To see this, enter the Dir command:

```
dir
```

DOS displays a report for the diskette in drive A, not the hard disk in drive C:

```
Volume in drive A is FRED
Volume Serial Number is 1861-674C
Directory of A:\

File not found

A:>_
```

FRED is the name you gave the diskette when you formatted it. *File not found* is how DOS tells you that the diskette is formatted but contains no files.

You'll need some files for the next few examples; the quickest way to get some files on the diskette is to copy them from the hard disk. Type the following to copy all the files whose name starts with D and whose extension is HLP from the directory named \DOS on your hard disk to the diskette in drive A:

```
copy c:\dos\d*.hlp
```

You don't have to type the drive letter for the diskette drive because unless you tell it otherwise, the Copy command assumes you want to copy to the current drive.

DOS displays the name of each file as it is copied. When all the files have been copied, DOS tells you how many files it copied and returns to the command prompt. The screen should look like this:

```
C:\DOS\DEFRAG.HLP
C:\DOS\DOSSHELL.HLP
C:\DOS\DOSHELP.HLP
C:\DOS\DBLSPACE.HLP
        4 file(s) copied
```

Confirm that the files were transferred by typing the Dir command again:

```
dir
```

Now the Dir command report shows four files on the diskette:

```
 Volume in drive A is FRED
 Volume Serial Number is 1861-674C
 Directory of A:\

DEFRAG   HLP     9227 12-06-92    6:00a
DOSSHELL HLP   161323 12-06-92    6:00a
DOSHELP  HLP     5744 12-06-92    6:00a
DBLSPACE HLP    35851 12-06-92    6:00a
        4 file(s)    212145 bytes
                    1243648 bytes free
```

Formatting a Diskette Quickly

When you format a diskette unconditionally, DOS deletes any files that are stored on the diskette and checks the surface of the disk for any defects that could prevent the reliable storing of data. These steps take time and aren't really necessary, unless you suspect that the surface of the diskette might be damaged (DOS refers to damaged locations as *bad sectors*).

To save time, DOS lets you specify a quick format with the /Q parameter. A quick format doesn't really erase any files stored on the diskette, it simply erases the index to those files so that it *appears* that the files are gone; nor does a quick format check for bad sectors. Although the process takes much less time, to DOS the disk still appears to be empty.

Type the following to quick-format the diskette to which you just copied the four files:

```
format a: /q
```

Press enter twice. The response to a quick format is quite different from the earlier response you saw to the unconditional format. DOS adds a line to the output, doesn't keep track of the percent complete, and finishes the process in much less time:

```
Checking existing disk format.
Saving UNFORMAT information.
QuickFormatting 1.44M
Format complete.

Volume label (11 characters, ENTER for none)?
```

The second line, Saving UNFORMAT information, tells you that DOS is saving information that will let you restore the disk to its previous (before formatting) status. DOS now is waiting for you to type the volume label; type sales. Now DOS displays the statistics about the newly formatted disk's capacity:

```
1457664 bytes total disk space
1457664 bytes available on disk
    512 bytes in each allocation unit.
   2847 allocation units available on disk.

Volume Serial Number is 192D-18E9

QuickFormat another (Y/N)?
```

You're through formatting disks, so press n. To see the result of your efforts, once again check the contents of the diskette in drive A by typing the Dir command:

```
dir

 Volume in drive A is SALES
 Volume Serial Number is 192D-18E9
 Directory of A:\

File not found

A:\>
```

Just as when you checked the diskette after formatting it the first time, it's empty. Quick-formatting the diskette erased the files you copied to it.

Unformatting a Diskette

But what if you didn't really mean to format this diskette? What if you really needed those files? This isn't as hypothetical as it sounds; some of the worst computer errors are, in fact, people errors. We tell the computer to do the wrong thing, and it dutifully does the wrong thing. (Cynics allege that the primary contribution of computers is to let us make mistakes much more quickly than we ever could before.)

DOS does try to protect us against ourselves. If you catch the mistake before you store any other files on the diskette and if you didn't unconditionally format the diskette, you can get those files back with the Unformat command. Type the following:

```
unformat a:
```

DOS responds by asking you to put the diskette to unformat (or, as DOS puts it, to *rebuild*) in drive A:

```
Insert disk to rebuild in drive A:
and press ENTER when ready.
```

The diskette is already there, so press Enter. Now DOS warns you to make certain that this is the diskette you want to unformat and gives you a chance to change your mind:

```
Restores the system area of your disk by using the image file created
by the MIRROR command.

   WARNING !!        WARNING !!

This command should be used only to recover from the inadvertent use of
the FORMAT command or the RECOVER command.  Any other use of the UNFORMAT
command may cause you to lose data!  Files modified since the MIRROR image
file was created may be lost.

Searching disk for MIRROR image.

The last time the MIRROR or FORMAT command was used was at 18:20 on 10-16-93.

The MIRROR image file has been validated.

Are you sure you want to update the system area of your drive A (Y/N)?
```

Press Y to continue (if you press any other key, DOS ends the process and returns to the command prompt without altering the contents of the diskette). Now DOS recovers the files that appeared to be erased when you quick-formatted the disk, telling you when it has finished:

```
The system area of drive A has been rebuilt.
You may need to restart the system.
A:\>
```

You don't have to restart the system; that message applies when you unformat the disk from which you normally start DOS.

Now type `dir` to see if the files are back. You should see the same four files that DOS reported earlier:

```
Volume in drive A is FRED
Volume Serial Number is 192D-18D6
Directory of A:\

DEFRAG   HLP        9227 12-06-92    6:00a
DOSSHELL HLP      161323 12-06-92    6:00a
DOSHELP  HLP        5744 12-06-92    6:00a
DBLSPACE HLP       35851 12-06-92    6:00a
         4 file(s)       212145 bytes
                        1243648 bytes free
```

Creating a System Diskette

If you turn your system on when there's a diskette in drive A and the drive latch (if there is one) is closed, the system tries to start DOS from the diskette. If the diskette doesn't contain the files that DOS needs to begin, you'll see a message telling you that DOS can't begin.

To see this, make sure that the diskette you've been working with is still in drive A and press Ctrl+Alt+Del to restart your system (hold down the keys labeled *Ctrl* and *Alt*, then press and release the key labeled *Del*). The system should act as if it's starting, then stop and display this message:

```
Non-System disk or disk error
Replace and press any key when ready
```

Remove the diskette; or, if there is a drive latch, flip it open, and press any key. Now DOS starts as it always does, because the files that DOS needs are on your hard disk, transferred there when DOS was installed. If DOS starts the Shell, choose *Exit* from the File menu to return to the command prompt; when DOS displays the command prompt, whether or not you had to exit the Shell, close the A drive door and type `a:` to make drive A the current drive.

What if your hard disk fails or one of the files that DOS needs is changed in such a way that DOS won't run properly? How can you run DOS without your hard disk?

With the Format command, you can create a system diskette that will start DOS. The /S (for *system*) parameter tells DOS to format the diskette and then copy the files needed to start DOS from the hard disk to the diskette.

Try it; the diskette you have been using for the examples in this chapter should still be in drive A; type the following:

```
format a: /s
```

When DOS prompts you to insert the new diskette for drive A, press Enter. The responses are the same as in the earlier examples, with one exception: DOS displays *System transferred* after formatting is complete and before it prompts you to enter a volume label:

```
Checking existing disk format.
Saving UNFORMAT information.
Verifying 1.44M
Format complete.
System transferred

Volume label (11 characters, ENTER for none)?
```

You'll be able to start your system using this diskette, so type dos6 system. As before, DOS concludes by showing the vital statistics:

```
   1457664 bytes total disk space
    132096 bytes used by system
   1325568 bytes available on disk

       512 bytes in each allocation unit.
      2589 allocation units available on disk.

Volume Serial Number is 1CB5-13D3

Format another (Y/N)?
```

This time, there's a new entry that tells you how much space the system files take up, reducing the storage available on the diskette by that amount. You're through formatting diskettes, so type n. Now type dir to check the directory of files on the diskette. DOS shows one file, COMMAND.COM.

But two other DOS files were copied. They're different from most other files; they're *system* files, which DOS doesn't normally show in the list of files. You can tell the Dir command to let you see these files, however, by specifying the /A (for *attributes*) parameter and a one-letter code that identifies the attribute you're interested in:

A   Archive (this file has changed and should be archived)

D   Directory (this file is actually a subdirectory that contains other files)

H   Hidden (DOS doesn't normally show this file in a directory listing)

R   Read-only (this file can't be changed or deleted)

S   System (a file used by DOS that isn't normally shown in a directory listing)

You can check or change any of these file attributes with the Attribute command or display their directory entry by using the /A parameter with the Dir command. To see the directory entries for the files with the S (for *system*) attribute, type this Dir command:

```
dir /as
```

Now DOS shows you just the system files:

```
Volume in drive A is DOS6 SYSTEM
Volume Serial Number is 1CB5-13D3
Directory of A:\

IO        SYS     40038 12-06-92    6:00a
MSDOS     SYS     37480 12-06-92    6:00a
        2 file(s)        77518 bytes
                       1307136 bytes free
```

These two files, plus the one you saw a moment ago (COMMAND.COM), are the three files that are required to start DOS. Although many other files are needed to supply all the DOS features and commands, this minimum set lets you start the system if something should happen to your hard disk.

Copying an Entire Diskette

You used the Copy command in this chapter to copy four files from the hard disk to a diskette. You can copy all the files in a directory — or all the files on a disk — with a single command. This doesn't necessarily create a duplicate of the disk from which you copied the files, however, because DOS might arrange the files more compactly in the process of copying them from one disk to another.

The Diskcopy command lets you make an exact duplicate of a diskette, no matter how the files might be stored. Both diskettes must be the same type and capacity; you'll probably use the same diskette drive for the original and the copy, so DOS prompts you to swap the original (DOS calls it the *source*) and the copy (DOS calls it the *target*) until the process is complete.

To make a duplicate of the system diskette you just created, type the following:

```
diskcopy a: a:
```

The command specifies two drive letters; the first is the drive that will contain the original, and the second is the drive that will hold the new copy. Notice that you specified drive A for both drives. If your system has two drives of the same type, you can specify different drive letters, but specifying the same drive letter works no matter how many diskette drives you have.

DOS responds by asking you to put the original diskette in drive A:

```
Insert SOURCE diskette in drive A:
Press any key to continue . . .
```

The system diskette you just created should still be in drive A, so press a key (the space bar is handy). DOS starts reading the contents of the diskette into memory; when it has read as much as it can, it prompts you to put in the diskette that is to receive the copy:

```
Insert TARGET diskette in drive A:
Press any key to continue . . .
```

Remove the system diskette and put in either a new diskette or one that doesn't contain any files that you need; then press Enter. DOS copies the files it read into memory to the new diskette (if the diskette isn't formatted, DOS formats it first). When it has written all the files it read, it prompts you to put the original system diskette (the *SOURCE*) back in and press any key. Do so, then put the copy in when it prompts you to swap again. Continue swapping diskettes until DOS prompts you that the copy is complete.

The diskettes should now be identical. You can't be sure that two diskettes are identical even if their directory listings are the same, because files could be stored in different locations on the diskettes. DOS includes the Diskcomp command, however, which compares the exact contents of two diskettes; it doesn't just make sure the name and length of each file stored on the disks are the same; it compares each byte of each diskette to make sure they're identical. The Diskcomp command prompts you to swap the two diskettes to be compared, just as the Diskcopy command prompts you to swap the original and the copy.

You don't have to go through the exercise of comparing your two system diskettes: Rest assured, if you did the examples properly, they're identical. Write `DOS 6.0 startup disk` on the label of each diskette and store them in a safe place. In Chapter 12, you'll work with your CONFIG.SYS and AUTOEXEC.BAT files. When you have these files the way you want them, add them to these disks and make them your emergency system diskettes.

Chapter Review

You prepared a diskette for use using several of the options of the Format command; you should now be comfortable preparing a floppy disk for use. The most important points covered in this chapter:

- Before you can use a new diskette, you must prepare it with the Format command.

- If a diskette is write-protected, you can't change or delete files stored on it.

- Formatting a diskette unconditionally (the /U parameter) deletes any files stored on the diskette.

- Quick-formatting a diskette (the /Q parameter) does not delete existing files; you can recover the files it contained when it was formatted by unformatting it with the Unformat command before any new files are stored on it.

- You can create a system diskette—one you can use to start your computer—by formatting the diskette with the Format command and the /S (for *system*) parameter.

- The /AS (for *attribute system*) parameter of the Dir command displays just the system files in a directory listing.

CHAPTER

11

MANAGING YOUR FILES
WITH DOS COMMANDS

In the previous two chapters, you used a few DOS commands to see which files were stored in a directory (Dir), to change the current directory (CD), and to display the contents of a file (Type). In this chapter you'll work more with the DOS commands that let you manage your files.

If you're continuing from Chapter 9, the root directory should be the current directory. If you're starting your system, exit the Shell if necessary, and make sure that the root directory is the current directory—the command prompt should be *C:\>*—if it isn't, type cd \ (remember, the backslash is the name that DOS uses for the root directory).

Displaying the Directory Tree

As you saw in earlier chapters, the Shell's directory tree gives you a pretty clear picture of the directory structure on your disk, showing which directories are contained in which. The Dir command, on the other hand, simply lists the files and directories in a particular directory. For example, type dir to display the list of directories and files in the root directory:

```
Volume in drive C is MS-DOS_6
Volume Serial Number is 198C-7A04
Directory of C:\

WORD         <DIR>       10-16-93    2:16p
MENU         <DIR>       10-16-93    2:21p
DOS          <DIR>       10-16-93   10:58a
BATCH        <DIR>       10-16-93    2:27p
ACCOUNTS     <DIR>       10-16-93    7:31p
COMMAND  COM     53405 12-06-92     6:00a
AUTOEXEC BAT       365 10-16-93     1:15p
CONFIG   SYS       615 10-16-93     8:59p
WINA20   386      9349 12-06-92     6:00a
         9 file(s)      63734 bytes
                     16780909 bytes free
```

Your screen won't look exactly like this, of course, but chances are it includes the directories named ACCOUNTS (if you did the examples in the Shell part of the book) and DOS, and files named CONFIG.SYS, AUTOEXEC.BAT, and COMMAND.COM.

This list is informative, but not nearly as descriptive as the picture that the Shell's directory tree gives you. DOS can get a bit more graphic, though. The Tree command displays the directory structure of the current directory and all the directories it contains. The root directory is the current directory, so the Tree command shows the directory structure of your entire hard disk. Try it; type `tree`; DOS displays your directory structure:

```
Directory PATH listing for Volume MS-DOS_6
Volume Serial Number is 198C-7A04
C:\
├─── WORD
├─── MENU
├─── DOS
├─── BATCH
└─── ACCOUNTS
         └──CHARTS
               └──HISTORY
```

You can't choose a directory from the display as you can in the Shell. All you can do it look at it, but the diagram does give you a better picture of how the directories on your disk are organized than the Dir command output does. Like the Shell's directory tree, the relationship of the directories is shown by indenting subordinate directories and drawing a line from the beginning of each subdirectory to the bottom of the directory that contains it.

If your hard disk has more directories than will fit in one screenful, the top of the tree scrolls out of sight before the bottom appears. You can momentarily halt the scrolling by pressing the Pause key, but DOS gives you a couple of ways to look at long displays more conveniently.

Viewing Long Output with More

In an earlier example, you used the /P (for *pause*) parameter of the Dir command to display a long directory listing one screenful at a time. The More command lets you view almost any long output the same way; it displays the first screenful of output and then displays *--More--* at the bottom of the screen and waits for you to press a key before displaying the next screenful.

The More command is one of a group of commands called *filters*, because you pass the output of a command through them (like water though a filter) on the way to the screen or a file. Continuing the waterworks analogy, channeling the output of a command to a filter is called *piping*, and the connection itself is referred to as a *pipe*.

To see how this works, you'll pipe the output of the Tree command to the More command. To make sure that the output is more than one screenful, you'll include the /F parameter with the Tree command, to add the name of each file on the disk to the output; type the following (the ¦ is above the backslash on the keyboard):

```
tree /f ¦ more
```

You should see the first screenful of the output of the Tree command, this time including the file names. The last line reads *--More--*; press any key to see the next screenful. If you want to cancel the command and return to the command prompt before you reach the end of the output, press Ctrl+Break.

You can also use the More command to view a long file. You displayed a file using the Type command in an earlier chapter; type the following to display the file named DOSHELP.HLP, piping the output to More:

```
type c:\dos\doshelp.hlp ¦ more
```

Again, DOS displays the first screenful, then waits for you to press a key before displaying the next screenful:

```
@ Copyright (C) 1990-1993 Microsoft Corp.  All rights reserved.
@ This is the DOS general help file.  It contains a brief
@ description of each command supported by the DOS help command.
@ Type DOSHELP with no arguments to display the text in this file.
@ Lines beginning with @ are comments, and are ignored by DOSHELP.
@ This file may be modified to add new commands.  If the DOSHELP command-name
@ form is to be used, any new commands should support the /? parameter.
@ New commands should start in the first column.  Any extra lines needed
@ for a command description should be preceded by white space.  Commands
@ must be added in alphabetical order.
APPEND    Allows programs to open data files in specified directories as if
          they were in the current directory.
ATTRIB    Displays or changes file attributes.
BREAK     Sets or clears extended CTRL+C checking.
CALL      Calls one batch program from another.
CD        Displays the name of or changes the current directory.
CHCP      Displays or sets the active code page number.
CHDIR     Displays the name of or changes the current directory.
CHKDSK    Checks a disk and displays a status report.
CLS       Clears the screen.
COMMAND   Starts a new instance of the MS-DOS command interpreter.
COPY      Copies one or more files to another location.
CTTY      Changes the terminal device used to control your system.
DATE      Displays or sets the date.
```

Press any key to see the next screenful. Unless you want to read the entire file, press Ctrl+Break to cancel the command.

The More command is a fairly simple solution, but you still can only move toward the end of the output. Sometimes it would really be handy to be able to scroll back and forth. Here's a technique that lets you do just that.

Redirecting Command Output to a File

DOS commands such as Tree and Dir normally display their output on the screen. You can, however, tell DOS to store the output in a file instead of displaying it. This is called *redirecting* the output of a command, because you're changing the direction of the output from the screen to a file.

Just as you used a special symbol (¦) to tell DOS to pipe command output to a filter, you use a special symbol to redirect command output. The symbol for redirecting command output is the greater-than symbol (>), because it looks something like an arrow pointing toward whatever follows it.

To redirect the output of the Tree command into a file named TREE.TXT, type the following:

```
tree > tree.txt
```

You don't see much when you press Enter after this command, although you may hear some disk activity. DOS doesn't display the directory tree because you told it to put that output in a file named TREE.TXT instead of displaying it.

Now you'll use the DOS Editor to look at the file TREE.TXT (you saw the DOS Editor earlier in the book, while you were working with the Shell). Type the following to start the Editor and load the file TREE.TXT:

```
edit tree.txt
```

The Editor displays the first screenful of the Tree command output; it should look something like this:

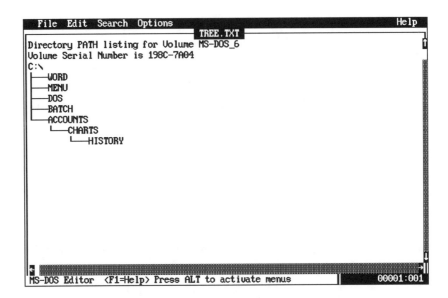

Now you can scroll through the output using the arrow keys, the PgDn and PgUp keys, or your mouse. You can even add comments, print it, and hang it on your wall as a map to where your information is stored. When you're through with the directory tree, choose *Exit* from the File menu to return to DOS.

Note

When you redirect command output to a file, DOS creates the file you specify, if it doesn't exist. If a file by that name does exist, however, DOS replaces its contents with the command output you're redirecting. For this reason, when you're redirecting command output, be sure not to specify the name of a file you want to keep because you'll lose whatever it contains.

In addition to the /F (for *Files*) parameter, the Tree command has another parameter that you might find useful if you're going to print its output. The /A (for *ASCII*) parameter replaces the graphic characters used to create the smooth lines showing the tree structure with standard keyboard characters, such as dashes, plus signs, and vertical bars. If your printer can't print the graphic characters, use the /A parameter to create a file that any printer can print.

Controlling Which Files Dir Lists

When you were using the Shell, you used settings in the File Display Options dialog box to control which files appeared in the file list. You listed a single file by specifying its name; you listed a group of files that had the same name or extension by using the wildcard character (*). You can control the output of the Dir command in much the same way.

For the next few examples you'll be working in the DOS directory, so type the following to change the current directory to \DOS:

```
cd dos
```

To display the directory listing for just the file DOSSHELL.HLP, for example, type the following:

```
dir dosshell.hlp
```

DOS displays just one directory entry:

```
 Volume in drive C is MS-DOS_6
 Volume Serial Number is 198C-7A04
 Directory of C:\DOS

DOSSHELL HLP     161323 12-06-92   6:00a
        1 file(s)      161323 bytes
                    16762880 bytes free
```

As you saw in the previous chapter, you can also use the same wildcard characters you used in the Shell to specify which files to include in the output. Type the following to list all the files whose name is DOSSHELL, regardless of their extension:

```
dir dosshell.*
```

Now DOS shows you the entries for seven files:

```
Volume in drive C is MS-DOS_6
Volume Serial Number is 198C-7A04
Directory of C:\DOS

DOSSHELL VID      9462 12-06-92    6:00a
DOSSHELL COM      4620 12-06-92    6:00a
DOSSHELL GRB      4421 12-06-92    6:00a
DOSSHELL EXE    236378 12-06-92    6:00a
DOSSHELL HLP    161323 12-06-92    6:00a
DOSSHELL INI     17808 10-16-93    5:30p
        6 file(s)      434012 bytes
                     16764928 bytes free
```

Instead of specifying all files with a particular name, regardless of extension, you can specify all files with a particular extension, regardless of name. Type the following to see all the files whose name starts with D and whose extension is HLP:

```
dir *.hlp
```

This time, DOS finds four files:

```
Volume in drive C is MS-DOS_6
Volume Serial Number is 198C-7A04
Directory of C:\DOS

DEFRAG   HLP      9227 12-06-92    6:00a
DOSSHELL HLP    161323 12-06-92    6:00a
DOSHELP  HLP      5744 12-06-92    6:00a
DBLSPACE HLP     35851 12-06-92    6:00a
        4 file(s)      212145 bytes
                     16764928 bytes free
```

The more files a directory contains, the more useful these options of the Dir command become when you're trying to find a particular file.

As you've probably already noticed, the Dir command always adds up the total number of bytes in the listed files; it also tells you how many bytes are unused in the current directory.

Creating a New Directory

You added several new directories to your hard disk while you were using the Shell. The MD (*Make Directory*) command lets you do the same. Unless you tell it otherwise, the MD command creates the new directory within the current directory. You're going to create a directory in the root directory, so before typing the CD command, you're going to make the root directory the current directory.

But don't type the CD command to change the current directory just yet. You may have noticed that the Dir command output shows some odd entries in each directory, except the root. These two entries consist of one period (.) and two periods (..) and are followed by *<DIR>*, identifying them as directories. These don't represent actual directories. They are symbolic entries that DOS uses to represent the current directory (.) and the directory that contains the current directory (..). To change to the directory that contains the current directory—sometimes called the *parent* of the current directory—you specify the name as two periods. Type the following to change to the root directory (the parent of DOS):

```
cd ..
```

Now create a directory named BUDGETS in the root directory by typing the following:

```
md budgets
```

Creating a new directory doesn't change the curent directory: the system prompt (*C:\>*) shows you that the current directory is still the root.

You can create a directory in a directory that isn't the current directory by including the complete path of the directory names, starting with the root. For example, type the following to create a directory named SALES in the directory you just created named BUDGETS, which is in the root:

```
md \budgets\sales
```

Now type tree to see your two new directories:

```
Directory PATH listing for Volume MS-DOS_6
Volume Serial Number is 198C-7A04
C:\
├─── WORD
├─── MENU
├─── DOS
├─── BATCH
├─── ACCOUNTS
│       └─── CHARTS
│               └─── HISTORY
└─── BUDGETS
        └─── SALES
```

Copying Files

In the previous chapter, you copied some files to your newly formatted diskette. Now that you have a couple of new directories, you can
try some variations of the Copy command.

The general form of the Copy command is:

copy *source* [*target*]

The *source*, which is the name of the file or files to be copied, is required; the *target* is optional, which is why it's shown in brackets. If
you don't specify the target, DOS copies the file or files to the current directory.

First, you'll copy the file DOSSHELL.INI from the directory
named DOS to the directory named BUDGETS without leaving
the current directory. Type the following:

```
copy c:\dos\dosshell.ini c:\budgets
```

You specified just the target directory's path name (*c:\budgets*) because you want to keep the same file name; if you wanted to give the
copy of the file a different name, you would specify the new name as
part of the target parameter. Try it; copy DOSSHELL.INI from
\DOS again, but call this copy WORKING.DOC:

```
copy c:\dos\dosshell.ini c:\budgets\working.doc
```

Now, check what you've accomplished by listing the contents of
the Budgets directory; type the following:

```
dir \budgets
```

Budgets contains one subdirectory and two files (plus those two
symbolic entries):

```
Volume in drive C is MS-DOS_6
Volume Serial Number is 198C-7A04
Directory of C:\BUDGETS

.              <DIR>       10-16-93    7:29p
..             <DIR>       10-16-93    7:29p
SALES          <DIR>       10-16-93    7:29p
DOSSHELL INI     17808     10-16-93    5:30p
WORKING  DOC     17808     10-16-93    5:30p
        5 file(s)          35616 bytes
                        16721920 bytes free
```

Just as you use the wildcard character (*) to display a group of files with the same name or extension, you can also use it to copy a group of files. For example, suppose you wanted to copy all files whose extension is HLP from the directory named DOS to the directory named BUDGETS; type the following to make \BUDGETS the current directory and copy the files:

```
cd budgets
copy c:\dos\*.hlp
```

Because Budgets is the current directory, you didn't have to include a target in the Copy command. DOS responds by naming each file as it is copied, then tells you how many files it copied:

```
C:\DOS\APPNOTES.TXT
C:\DOS\README.TXT
        2 file(s) copied
```

If you check the results by typing dir, you'll find a total of seven files in \BUDGETS:

```
Volume in drive C is MS-DOS_6
Volume Serial Number is 198C-7A04
Directory of C:\BUDGETS

.              <DIR>        10-16-93    7:29p
..             <DIR>        10-16-93    7:29p
SALES          <DIR>        10-16-93    7:29p
DOSSHELL INI      17808     10-16-93    5:30p
WORKING  DOC      17808     10-16-93    5:30p
APPNOTES TXT       9058     12-06-92    6:00a
README   TXT      42618     12-06-92    6:00a
        7 file(s)        87292 bytes
                      16664576 bytes free
```

Remember, only five of those are actually files or directories; the other two are the symbolic entries . and .., representing the current and parent directories.

Moving Files To a Different Location

Often you don't want two copies of the same file—the original and a copy—you want to move the original to a different location. That's what the Move command does: Unlike the Copy command, it makes a copy of the file in the target directory or disk, then deletes the original.

The Move command follows the same general form as the Copy command (except you always must specify the target of a move). For example, to move the files APPNOTES.TXT and README.TXT from \BUDGETS to \BUDGETS\SALES, type the following:

```
move *.txt sales
```

DOS responds by showing you the old and new locations of the file:

```
c:\budgets\appnotes.txt => c:\budgets\sales\appnotes.txt [ok]
c:\budgets\readme.txt => c:\budgets\sales\readme.txt [ok]
```

Use the Dir command to confirm that the files are gone from the current directory:

```
Volume in drive C is MS-DOS_6
Volume Serial Number is 198C-7A04
Directory of C:\BUDGETS

.               <DIR>        10-16-93   10:14p
..              <DIR>        10-16-93   10:14p
SALES           <DIR>        10-16-93   10:14p
DOSSHELL INI     17808 10-16-93   10:14p
WORKING  DOC     17808 10-16-93   10:14p
         5 file(s)        35616 bytes
                    16633856 bytes free
```

The files whose extension is TXT are gone. Now check the directory of \BUDGETS\SALES to confirm that the files were moved:

```
dir sales

Volume in drive C is MS-DOS_6
Volume Serial Number is 198C-7A04
Directory of C:\BUDGETS\SALES

.               <DIR>        10-16-93   10:14p
..              <DIR>        10-16-93   10:14p
APPNOTES TXT      9058 12-06-92    6:00a
README   TXT     42618 12-06-92    6:00a
         4 file(s)        51676 bytes
                    16635904 bytes free
```

DOS moved the files, just as you specified. Now move them back, using the single-dot symbolic reference for the current directory; again, DOS shows you the old and new locations of the files. Type another Move command:

```
move sales\*.* .
c:\budgets\sales\appnotes.txt => c:\budgets\appnotes.txt [ok]
c:\budgets\sales\readme.txt => c:\budgets\readme.txt [ok]
```

Confirm that they're back by typing dir:

```
Volume in drive C is MS-DOS_6
Volume Serial Number is 198C-7A04
Directory of C:\BUDGETS

.              <DIR>        10-16-93   10:14p
..             <DIR>        10-16-93   10:14p
SALES          <DIR>        10-16-93   10:14p
DOSSHELL INI     17808 10-16-93   10:14p
WORKING  DOC     17808 10-16-93   10:14p
APPNOTES TXT      9058 12-06-92    6:00a
README   TXT     42618 12-06-92    6:00a
        7 file(s)        87292 bytes
                      16633856 bytes free
```

Exercise some care when you use the Move command. Like the Copy command, Move erases an existing file if you specify its name as the target of the move.

Deleting Files You No Longer Need

The Del (Delete) command deletes one or more files from a disk. Type the following to delete the file named WORKING.DOC from the current directory:

```
del working.doc
```

DOS doesn't acknowledge the Del command; it just displays the command prompt.

Just as you copied files to and from a directory other than the current directory by including the path of directory names before the file name, you can delete files from any directory. Type the following to change to the root directory and delete all the remaining files in the directory named BUDGETS:

```
cd \
del \budgets
```

By not specifying a file name at all, just the name of a directory, you're telling DOS to delete all the files in the directory. Because deleting all the files in a directory is a pretty drastic measure, DOS wants to be sure you really mean it:

```
All files in directory will be deleted!
Are you sure (Y/N)? _
```

DOS wants you to confirm the wholesale deletion. Confirm the deletion by pressing Y, then Enter. As before, DOS deletes the files with no acknowledgment other than the sound of some disk activity and displaying the command prompt again.

Change the current directory back to \BUDGETS by typing cd budgets.

Undeleting Files You Accidentally Deleted

It will happen, if it hasn't already. No matter how dumb it sounds, you're going to tell DOS to delete a file you don't want to delete. At least once. And DOS will do it. Just accept that.

But all isn't lost, because DOS doesn't really *erase* a file when you get rid of it with the Del command; it simply changes the first letter of the file's name to a question mark and removes the file's entry from the directory listing. The file is still there, but the space on the disk where it is stored is now available for storing other files. Until DOS stores another file in that space, you can restore the file with the Undelete command. You can't tell exactly when DOS will store another file in the deleted file's space, but it will probably be the next time you copy a file or use a program like a word processor or spreadsheet, because DOS has to store the new or revised file you work on. The sooner you try to restore the file, the better your chance of success.

For starters, you can use Undelete with the /LIST parameter to see a list of files deleted from the current directory that you can restore. Type the following:

```
undelete /list
```

DOS displays a list of six files (the ones you just deleted):

```
UNDELETE - A delete protection facility
Copyright (C) 1987-1993 Central Point Software, Inc.
All rights reserved.

Directory: C:\BUDGETS
File Specifications: *.*

    Delete Sentry control file not found.

    Deletion-tracking file not found.

    MS-DOS directory contains    4 deleted files.
    Of those,    4 files may be recovered.

Using the MS-DOS directory method.

    ?OSSHELL INI    17808 10-16-93  5:30p  ...A
    ?ORKING  DOC    17808 10-16-93  5:30p  ...A
    ?PPNOTES TXT     9058 12-06-92  6:00a  ...A
    ?EADME   TXT    42618 12-06-92  6:00a  ...A
```

Remember, when you delete a file, DOS changes the first letter of the file name to a question mark. You don't have to display this list before attempting to undelete a file, but it does tell you whether there's a chance to restore it.

Undeleting a Single File

Suppose you want to recover just the file that was named WORK-ING.DOC (now ?ORKING.DOC). Simply include that file name with the UNDELETE command; type the following:

```
undelete working.doc
```

DOS responds with a display that tells you the file you specified can be undeleted, then asks you if you want to undelete it:

```
Directory: C:\BUDGETS
File Specifications: WORKING.DOC

    Delete sentry control file not found.

    Deletion-tracking file not found.

    MS-DOS directory contains    1 deleted files.
    Of those,    1 files may be recovered.

Using the MS-DOS directory.

    ?ORKING   DOC    17808  10-16-93  5:30p  ...A
Undelete (Y/N)?
```

Press Y. Now DOS asks you what the first letter of the file name should be (even though you included it when you typed the Undelete command):

```
Please type the first character for ?ORKING .DOC:
```

Press W. DOS restores the file and tells you about it:

```
File successfully undeleted.
```

A quick check of the directory shows that the file is back. Type dir:

```
Volume in drive C is MS-DOS_6
Volume Serial Number is 198C-7A04
Directory of C:\BUDGETS

.              <DIR>      10-16-93    7:29p
..             <DIR>      10-16-93    7:29p
SALES          <DIR>      10-16-93    7:29p
WORKING  DOC      17808 01-19-93    5:30p
         4 file(s)        17808 bytes
                      16732160 bytes free
```

Undeleting All the Files in a Directory

What if you wanted to undelete all the files that could be undeleted from the directory? Simply type the command with no parameters:

```
undelete
```

This time, the command finds files it can undelete; it starts by asking you whether to undelete the first:

```
Directory: C:\BUDGETS
File Specifications: *.*

    Delete sentry control file not found.

    Deletion-tracking file not found.

    MS-DOS directory contains    3 deleted files.
    Of those,    3 files may be recovered.

Using the MS-DOS directory.

    ?OSSHELL INI     17808  10-16-93   5:30p  ...A
Undelete (Y/N)?
```

It will ask you the same question about each file. Press N for each one; none will be undeleted.

You can quickly undelete all the deleted files in the current directory with the /ALL parameter. This isn't necessarily the most convenient way to use the command, however, because you may not want to undelete all the files, and DOS changes the first character of each file name to #. You'll have to change the name of each file back to what it was before. It would probably be quicker to simply type undelete and respond to the prompt for each file, choosing the ones you want to undelete and assigning the correct first letters for the file names.

Changing a File's Name

Sometimes you'll want to change the name of a file—for instance, when the Undelete command changes the first character of each undeleted file's name to #. The Ren (Rename) command changes a file's name, extension, or both.

The command is pretty straightforward: the only parameters are the name of the file and the new name you want to give it. Right now, the only file in the current directory is WORKING.DOC. Type the following to change its name to TRIAL.DOC and confirm the change:

```
ren working.doc trial.doc
dir
```

Now the only file is named TRIAL.DOC:

```
Volume in drive C is MS-DOS_6
Volume Serial Number is 198C-7A04
Directory of C:\BUDGETS

.               <DIR>        10-16-93     7:29p
..              <DIR>        10-16-93     7:29p
SALES           <DIR>        10-16-93     7:29p
TRIAL    DOC       17808 01-19-93     5:30p
        4 file(s)        17808 bytes
                      16732160 bytes free
```

You can use the wildcard character (*) with the Ren command to rename a group of files, as long as you want to make the same change to all the files. For example, suppose you wanted to change the extension DOC to TXT for all files. There's only one file in the current directory, but the command would be the same no matter how many there were. Type the following to change the extension DOC to TXT for all files in the directory, then display the result:

```
ren *.doc *.txt
dir
```

The only thing that has changed is the extension of the file:

```
Volume in drive C is MS-DOS_6
Volume Serial Number is 198C-7A04
Directory of C:\BUDGETS

.              <DIR>        10-16-93    7:29p
..             <DIR>        10-16-93    7:29p
SALES          <DIR>        10-16-93    7:29p
TRIAL    TXT       17808 01-19-93    5:30p
         4 file(s)       17808 bytes
                   16732160 bytes free
```

Even though the Shell lets you change the names of directories as well as files, the Ren command renames only files. If you want to change the name of a directory, you'll have to use the Shell.

Deleting a Directory

This just about wraps up this chapter. You won't be needing the practice files and directories you created, so this last series of examples deletes them. The Del command doesn't delete directories, just files. You use either the RD (Remove Directory) or Deltree command to delete a directory. The difference between the commands is that RD deletes only an empty directory, but Deltree deletes a directory and any files or subdirectories it contains.

First, type the following to create one more directory named CHARTS in BUDGETS:

```
md charts
```

Now, to delete the directory named \BUDGETS\SALES, type the following:

```
rd sales
```

As when it deletes a file, DOS makes no special acknowledgement that it deleted the directory, it just displays the command prompt. However, as you'll see in a moment, DOS displays an error message if you try to use RD to delete a directory that isn't empty or one that doesn't exist, so you can take the absence of an error message as confirmation that the directory was deleted.

You can't delete the current directory, so type the following to change the current directory to the next higher one and delete BUDGETS:

```
cd ..
rd budgets
```

This time DOS objects:

```
Invalid path, not directory,
or directory not empty
```

You can't delete a directory if it contains any files, and BUDGETS contains both a file (TRIAL.TXT) and a subdirectory (CHARTS). You could use the RD command to delete CHARTS and the Del command to delete TRIAL.TXT, then another RD command to delete BUDGETS, but there's a quicker way: the Deltree command. It deletes a directory no matter what the directory contains; type the following:

```
deltree budgets
```

Because this is such a powerful command—Deltree deletes an entire branch of the directory tree, which could be your entire file structure—DOS wants you to confirm that you want to do what you said you wanted to do:

```
Delete directory "budgets" and all its subdirectories? [yn]
```

Press Y. DOS confirms what it does:

```
Deleting budgets...
```

Even though DOS gives you a chance to change your mind before carrying out the Deltree command, use it with great care. It's all too easy to get in a hurry and type a command that's not really what you mean.

Confirm that the directories are gone with the Tree command:

```
tree
```

The directory tree now shows neither Budgets nor Sales:

```
Directory PATH listing for Volume MS-DOS_6
Volume Serial Number is 198C-7A04
C:.
├──── WORD
├──── MENU
├──── DOS
├──── BATCH
└──── ACCOUNTS
          └──── CHARTS
                   └──── HISTORY
```

Chapter Review

This chapter showed you the commands and parameters you use most frequently to manage your files and directories. Although the Shell gives you a better picture of how your files and directories are organized and offers a more convenient way of handling most of the file housekeeping chores, sometimes a DOS command is the quickest way to get something done. The important points covered in this chapter:

- The Tree command displays a directory tree, similar to the one in the Shell, which shows the structure of the directories on a disk.

- The More filter command lets you view long output from any other command, one screenful at a time.

- You send the output of a command to a filter command with the pipe symbol (¦).

- You can redirect the output of a command from the screen to a file by using the output redirection symbol (>).

- You can use wildcards to control which files are affected by a command.

- The MD (Make Directory) command creates a new directory.

- The Copy command creates a duplicate copy of a file in a different directory, or in the same directory if you give the copy a different file name.

- The Del (Delete) command deletes one or more files from a disk.

- The MOVE command moves a file from one disk or directory to another. It can also be used to rename a directory.

- If you delete the wrong file, you can restore it with the Undelete command, as long as you haven't stored other files on the disk since deleting the file.

- The Ren (Rename) command changes a file's name.

- The RD (Remove Directory) command removes a directory from a disk. The directory must be empty (it can't contain any files or other directories).

- The Deltree command deletes a directory, including all the files and subdirectories it contains.

CHAPTER

12

USING THE DOS EDITOR

Word processors are the most commonly used programs on personal computers; it's estimated that a word processor is used some portion of the time on almost 80 percent of all computers. For writing and formatting documents, for incorporating graphics and checking your spelling, nothing beats a word processor.

But for many jobs that involve creating or revising text files, a word processor isn't required and can even be overkill. In fact, no matter how proficient you become at using your computer, no matter how many sophisticated application programs you get, you never outgrow your need for a simple text editor. That's precisely what the DOS Editor is: A small text editor program, quick to load and easy to use.

You started the Editor once or twice in earlier chapters; in this chapter you'll actually use the Editor to create and revise text files. You can start the Editor either from the Shell or from the command prompt; it's handier to use the Shell, so start the Shell.

For one of your practice files, you'll make a copy of a text file in the DOS directory. To make a copy of DOSHELP.HLP named DOSHELP.TXT, highlight DOS in the directory tree, then highlight DOSHELP.HLP in the file list. Choose *Copy* from the File menu, and when the Shell prompts you to enter the name of the copy, type `doshelp.txt`. The screen should look like this before you press Enter:

```
┌──────────────── Copy File ────────────────┐
│                                            │
│                                            │
│   From:    ┌DOSHELP.HLP──────────────┐     │
│            └─────────────────────────┘     │
│   To:      ┌doshelp.txt_─────────────┐     │
│            └─────────────────────────┘     │
│                                            │
│                                            │
│    ( OK )        ( Cancel )     ( Help )   │
└────────────────────────────────────────────┘
```

Press Enter to copy the file. As a final preparation, make the root directory the current directory by highlighting *C:* at the top of the directory tree.

Starting the Editor

As you saw earlier, the Shell gives you a choice of several different ways to start a program: You can choose the program from the program list (if it appears there); choose its program file from the file list; choose *Run* from the File menu and type the name of the program file; choose a file whose extension has been associated with the program; or drag a text file's name to the program file's name in the file list.

Start the Editor by choosing *Run* from the File menu. In the *Command Line* text area, type edit. Just as the other times you started the Editor, the opening screen welcomes you to the Editor and tells you to press Enter to look at something called the Survival Guide or press Esc to clear the screen. You'll get a chance to explore the Survival Guide in a moment; for now, press Esc.

> **Note**
>
> If, when you try to run the Shell, you see the message *Can not find file QBASIC.EXE* instead of the Editor screen, the file named QBASIC.EXE is missing from the DOS directory. You'll have to copy the file—it's on the DOS installation disk number 2—into the DOS directory before you can run the Editor.

The Editor screen looks something like the Shell screen. Menu names are listed across the top: *File, Search, Options*, and, at the far right, *Help*. Scroll bars are on the right and at the bottom of the text area, and the last line of the display shows the effect of pressing certain keys. Just as in the Shell, you can use the keyboard or the mouse to operate the program. The two numbers separated by a colon at the right side of the last line show the row and column number of the cursor location (right now the cursor is at the beginning of the first row: row 1, column 1).

Entering Text

To enter text, you just type it. Unlike a word processor, however, the Editor doesn't let you type complete paragraphs without deciding where to break the lines; whenever you want to end a line and start another, you have to press Enter. A line can be up to 255 characters long. Enter these four lines and press Enter after each one:

```
Line one
Line two
Line three
Line four
```

Now the cursor is at the beginning of the fifth line. Use the arrow keys to move the cursor up, down, right, and left through the text. Press the End key, and the cursor moves to the end of the line that contains the cursor; press Home, and the cursor moves to the beginning of the line that contains the cursor. If you check the numbers in the lower right corner, you'll see that they track the position of the cursor.

In addition to choosing commands with the mouse, as you do in the Shell, you can also use it to position the cursor by moving the mouse pointer to where you want the cursor to be and clicking the left mouse button.

To enter lines of text in the middle of some existing text, position the cursor at the point where you want the new text and start typing. For example, to add some text after the first two lines, position the cursor at the beginning of the third line and type the following (pressing Enter to end each line):

```
Line five
Line six
```

Now your file should look like this:

```
Line one
Line two
Line five
Line six
Line three
Line four
```

You'll take care of the sequence problem in a moment.

Editing Text

You wouldn't want to use the DOS Editor to write a novel, but it's ideal for creating and revising notes, memos, and the short text files used by DOS and other programs. For example, DOS uses two files named AUTOEXEC.BAT and CONFIG.SYS to hold commands that are carried out each time you start or restart the system; you can also create batch files—text files that contain DOS commands to be carried out as if you typed them.

Editing an existing file could include deleting text, adding new text, or changing existing text. You can move text from one place to another, and you can even copy text so that it appears in more than one place in the file.

You already inserted some lines of new text when you added lines five and six. Inserting text in the middle of a line is just about as simple; after you position the cursor where you want to insert the text, the only additional step required is to make sure the Editor knows that you want to insert some new text, not replace the text that's already there.

Suppose you want to insert the word *number* between the two words *Line* and *one* in the first line. First, move the cursor to the beginning of the word *one*. Now look at the cursor; it should be an underline, which means that the Editor will insert whatever you type. If it isn't, press the Ins key. Type `number` followed by a space (to separate the words). The first line should read:

```
Line number one
```

In addition to inserting text, you can also overstrike, or replace existing text, character for character. Move the cursor to the beginning of the word *Line* in the second line and press Ins. The cursor changes to a block, which tells you that whatever you type will overstrike. Type `Second` and check the result. The characters you typed weren't inserted at the beginning of the line; they replaced the characters that were there. Now the line reads:

```
Secondwo
```

The cursor is positioned over the *w*. Finish this change by pressing the space bar and typing `line`. Here's what your file should look like now:

```
Line number one
Second line
Line five
Line six
Line three
Line four
```

Moving and Copying Text

You can move or copy text from one place to another by selecting (highlighting) the text to be moved or copied and choosing the Copy, Cut, or Paste command from the Edit menu. These commands work in concert with a temporary storage area the Editor calls the *clipboard*.

- The Cut command puts a copy of the selected text in the clipboard and deletes the text from the file.

- The Copy command puts a copy of the selected text in the clipboard but leaves the text in the file.

- The Paste command puts a copy of the text in the clipboard in the file at the cursor position.

To move some text, then, you select the text to be moved, choose *Cut*, position the cursor at the new location, and choose *Paste*. To copy some text, you select the text, choose *Copy*, position the cursor at the new location, and choose *Paste*.

Note

As you work with these commands from the Edit menu, note the keyboard shortcut keys for each one: Cut is Shift+Del; Copy is Ctrl+Ins; and Paste is Shift+Ins. These keys are especially useful in the Editor, because you often don't want to take your hands off the keyboard when you're working with text.

Follow these steps to fix the sequence of lines by moving *Line five* and *Line six* to the end:

1. Move the cursor to the beginning of *Line five*.

2. Hold down the Shift key to tell the Editor you want to select some text and press the End key. The Editor highlights the entire line. (You can also use the mouse to select text: Position the cursor at the beginning of the text to be selected, hold down the left mouse button, and move the mouse across or down until the text you want to select is highlighted.)

3. Still holding down the Shift key, press the down arrow key, and both lines are highlighted all the way across the screen. You have selected the text to be moved.

4. Now choose *Cut* from the Edit menu. This is the unnerving part; you don't want to delete the text, you just want to move it, but it disappears. Not to worry, the text isn't gone, it's still on the clipboard.

5. Move the cursor to the beginning of the first line following *Line four*.

6. Choose *Paste* from the Edit menu.

Voilà! Your file should look like this:

```
Line number one
Second line
Line three
Line four
Line five
Line six
```

The process is almost the same to copy text; the only difference is that you choose *Copy* from the Edit menu instead of *Cut*. Follow these steps to copy the word *number* from the first line to the third line:

1. Move the cursor to the *n* in *number* in the first line.

2. Hold down the Shift key and then press the right arrow key until *number* and the space after it is highlighted.

3. Choose *Copy* from the Edit menu. Nothing much seems to happen but have faith.

4. Move the cursor to the *t* in *three* in the third line.

5. Choose *Paste* from the Edit menu.

Now your file should look like this:

```
Line number one
Second line
Line number three
Line four
Line five
Line six
```

When you paste text from the clipboard into a document, the text remains on the clipboard, so you can paste it as many times as you like. Check this out by pasting the word *number* in the appropriate spot in each of the next three lines, so that the file looks like this:

```
Line number one
Second line
Line number three
Line number four
Line number five
Line number six
```

This file is quite short, but cutting and pasting work the same way no matter how long a file is. Once you have cut or copied text to the clipboard, you can scroll anywhere in a file before you paste the text, without losing it.

Note

The Clear command in the Edit menu erases text from the file and *doesn't* put it on the clipboard; once you have deleted something using the Clear command (or the Del key), it's gone.

Saving Your File

The file on which you've been working exists only in the computer's memory. If the power failed or you turned your system off now, there would be no trace of the file. If you tried to exit the Editor without saving the file, however, the Editor would warn you and give you a chance to save it.

To save the file, choose *Save* from the File menu. The Editor displays the Save dialog box:

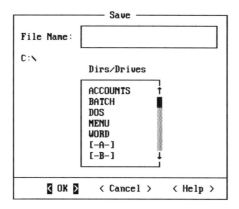

Type `sample.txt` and press Enter. The Editor saves the file on disk (in the root directory), clears the dialog box, and changes the title of the text area from *Untitled* to *SAMPLE.TXT*.

The Editor prompted you to enter a name because the file had no name; you just created it. From now on, whenever you choose *Save* from the File menu, the Editor replaces the version on disk with the version in memory without displaying a dialog box. If you wish, you can save a revised version of a file with a different name by choosing *Save As* from the File menu; the Editor then prompts you for a new name.

Getting Help

Like the Shell, the Editor offers online help information that can answer many of your questions right on the spot, saving you a trip to the manual. You get help in a couple of different ways.

If you press the right mouse button or F1 when no menu or command is highlighted, the Editor displays the Survival Guide you've seen mentioned several times. It's time you took a look at it instead of skipping it. Press the right mouse button, and the Editor displays the Survival Guide:

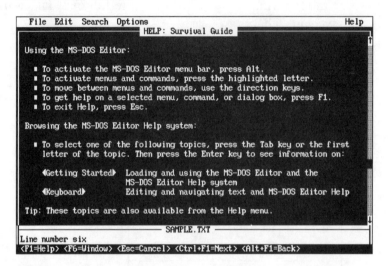

The Survival Guide is simply an introduction to the Editor that lets you choose one of the two major topics of the help system: *Getting Started* and *Keyboard*. These two topics, enclosed in green triangles, appear toward the bottom of the screen. You can choose either of them to get more information; double-click on *Getting Started*. Now the Editor displays the Getting Started help screen:

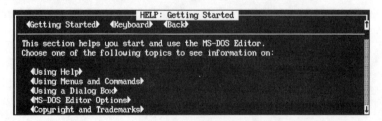

Here are five topics you can choose to see more detailed information. The top row of the help screen lets you choose the other major topic (*Keyboard*) or *Back*, which takes you back to the previous screen (the Survival Guide). Browse around in the help information, if you like. When you're through, press Esc to clear the screen and return to the normal Shell display.

If you press F1 while a command is highlighted or a dialog box is displayed, the Shell displays information specific to what you're doing. To see this, display the File menu, highlight the Open command, and press F1. The Shell displays the Open Command help screen:

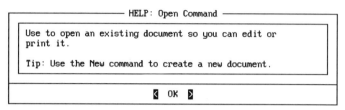

This is a pretty terse description of the Open command, but more detailed information is available. You'll make use of it in the last example of this chapter.

Opening a File

You've used some of the Editor commands to enter and revise some text. To see how you work with an existing file, you'll use the Open command from the File menu to load DOSHELP.TXT, the copy of DOSHELP.HLP you made at the beginning of the chapter.

Press Esc to remove the help screen, then press Enter to choose the Open command. The Editor displays the Open dialog box:

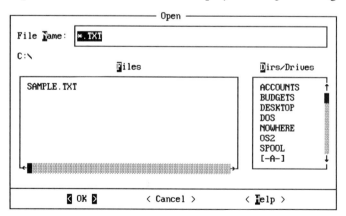

It may not be intuitively obvious what to do here. Now the Editor's help system gets a chance to shine; press F1 to see the Open Dialog help screen:

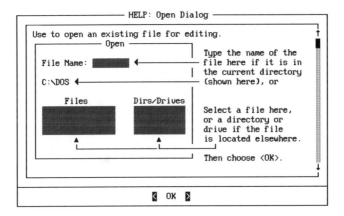

When you're reading a detailed help screen like this, sometimes it helps to switch back and forth between the help screen and the Editor screen by pressing Esc to switch to the Editor screen (the Open dialog box in this instance) and then F1 to see the help screen again.

As the help screen tells you, you can type the name of the file you want to open in the *File Name* field at the top of the dialog box or choose the name from the *Files* list in the middle of the dialog box. But the only file listed is SAMPLE.TXT (you may also see TREE .TXT if you didn't delete it after the exercises in Chapter 10); the file DOSHELP.TXT is in the directory named DOS.

But the help screen also told you that you can change the current drive or directory by choosing from the *Dirs/Drives* list at the right side of the dialog box. Sure enough, there's *DOS* about halfway down the list. Choose *DOS* to make it the current directory; now the dialog box should list three file names:

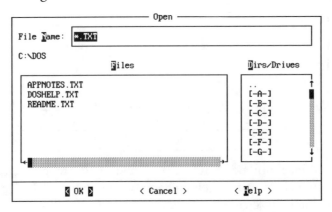

The second file, DOSHELP.TXT, is the one you want; choose it. If the Editor asks you if you want to save the current file, choose *No*. In a moment, the Editor displays the first screenful of DOSHELP .TXT:

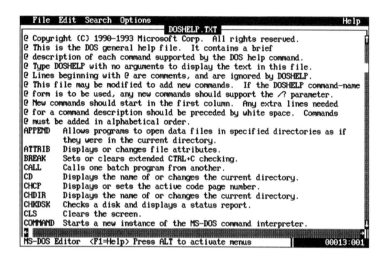

```
  File  Edit  Search  Options                                      Help
┌──────────────────────────────DOSHELP.TXT───────────────────────────────┐
│@ Copyright (C) 1990-1993 Microsoft Corp.  All rights reserved.        ▲│
│@ This is the DOS general help file.  It contains a brief              █│
│@ description of each command supported by the DOS help command.       █│
│@ Type DOSHELP with no arguments to display the text in this file.     █│
│@ Lines beginning with @ are comments, and are ignored by DOSHELP.     █│
│@ This file may be modified to add new commands.  If the DOSHELP command-name│
│@ form is to be used, any new commands should support the /? parameter.│
│@ New commands should start in the first column.  Any extra lines needed│
│@ for a command description should be preceded by white space.  Commands│
│@ must be added in alphabetical order.                                 │
│APPEND    Allows programs to open data files in specified directories as if│
│          they were in the current directory.                         │
│ATTRIB    Displays or changes file attributes.                        │
│BREAK     Sets or clears extended CTRL+C checking.                     │
│CALL      Calls one batch program from another.                       │
│CD        Displays the name of or changes the current directory.      │
│CHCP      Displays or sets the active code page number.               │
│CHDIR     Displays the name of or changes the current directory.      │
│CHKDSK    Checks a disk and displays a status report.                 │
│CLS       Clears the screen.                                          │
│COMMAND   Starts a new instance of the MS-DOS command interpreter.    ▼│
│■ ◄████████████████████████████████████████████████████████████████►  │
├─────────────────────────────────────────────────────────────────────┤
│MS-DOS Editor   <F1=Help> Press ALT to activate menus       00013:001 │
└─────────────────────────────────────────────────────────────────────┘
```

This file is much longer than the sample you created earlier in the chapter, but the editing commands work the same way. One Editor command you haven't used yet can be quite useful when you're working with longer files like this. Find, from the Search menu, searches the entire file for a word or phrase. This lets you quickly locate a line where you might want to make some changes.

Searching for and Replacing Text

Suppose you wanted to find some or all of the lines in this file that contained the word *directory*. Rather than scrolling through the file searching for the word, choose *Find* from the Search menu. The Editor displays the Find dialog box:

```
┌──────────────────────── Find ────────────────────────┐
│                                                       │
│ Find What: ┌───────────────────────────────────────┐ │
│            └───────────────────────────────────────┘ │
│                                                       │
│                                                       │
│     [ ] Match Upper/Lowercase        [ ] Whole Word   │
│                                                       │
├───────────────────────────────────────────────────────┤
│      ◄ OK ►          < Cancel >          < Help >     │
└───────────────────────────────────────────────────────┘
```

Type `directory` and press Enter. Almost instantly, the Editor highlights the word *directory* in the second line of the description of the Append command. The Search menu includes a Repeat Last Find command whose shortcut key is F3; press F3 to find the next occurrence, and the highlight jumps to the description of the CD command. Continue pressing F3 and you move through the file until you come to the last occurrence of *directory*, in the description of the Xcopy command. Press Esc to cancel the Find command.

What if you not only wanted to find a particular word or phrase, but you also wanted to change some or all of the occurrences to a different word or phrase? The Editor includes this capability, too. For example, to change some of the occurrences of *floppy disk* to *diskette*, choose *Change* from the Search menu; the Editor displays the Change dialog box. It already contains *directory* in the *Find What* field at the top of the box, because it remembers the last entry you specified for either Find or Change. Type `floppy disk`, press Tab, and type `diskette`. The dialog box should look like this:

```
┌──────────────────── Change ────────────────────┐
│                                                 │
│ Find What: │floppy disk                       │ │
│            └──────────────────────────────────┘ │
│ Change To: │diskette                          │ │
│            └──────────────────────────────────┘ │
│                                                 │
│   [ ] Match Upper/Lowercase     [ ] Whole Word  │
│                                                 │
├─────────────────────────────────────────────────┤
│ ◄ Find and Verify ► < Change All > < Cancel > < Help > │
└─────────────────────────────────────────────────┘
```

You don't want to change every occurrence, and you want to be able to choose whether to change each one, so tab to *<Find and Verify>* in the lower left corner. Now press Enter. The Editor highlights *floppy disk* in the description of Diskcomp (the Disk Compare command) and displays a smaller Change dialog box that lets you specify whether to: change this occurrence, skip it (leave it unchanged), cancel the whole command, or display help. Choose *Skip*; the Editor leaves *floppy disks* unchanged and highlights *floppy disk* in the next line, the Diskcopy command description. This time choose *Change*; the Editor changes *floppy disk* to *diskette*. The command ends at this point because these are the only two occurrences of *floppy disk* in the file. Press Enter again.

Exiting the Editor

Now you should have a pretty good feel for using the Editor. It's time to end this chapter, so choose *Exit* from the File menu. Because you have changed the open file and haven't saved the changed version, the Editor asks you if you want to save it now. You don't need the changed version, so choose *No.* The Editor screen goes away and you return to the Shell.

You no longer need DOSHELP.TXT in the DOS directory, so delete it (highlight DOSHELP.TXT in the file list and either press Del or choose *Delete* from the File menu). The Shell won't list SAMPLE.TXT until you start it again. To delete this file choose *Exit* from the File menu to leave the Shell. Then type the following (pressing Enter after each line):

```
cd..
del sample.txt
```

Chapter Review

The DOS Editor lets you quickly create or revise text files; although it lacks the capabilities of a word processor, it's ideal for many small jobs. The most important points covered in this chapter:

- The file named QBASIC.EXE must be in the DOS directory for the Editor to work.

- You use the cursor control keys—the arrows, PgUp, PgDn, Home, and End—to move around in a file.

- Pressing the Ins key alternates between between insert and overstrike (the cursor changes between an underline and a block).

- The Cut, Copy, and Paste commands from the Edit menu let you move and copy text from one place to another in a file.

- You can paste the same text into more than one place in a file.

- A line in the Editor can be up to 255 characters long.

- To save the file you're working on, choose *Save* from the File menu.

- To save the file you're working on with a different name, choose *Save As* from the File menu.

- If you press F1 when a command or dialog box is active, the Shell displays a help screen specific to what you're doing.

- If you press F1 or click the right mouse button when nothing is highlighted or active, the Shell displays the Survival Guide, a table of contents for the online help.

- To load a file into the Editor, choose *Open* from the File menu.

- The Find command in the Search menu lets you locate a word or phrase anywhere in the file.

- The Change command in the Search menu lets you locate a word or phrase anywhere in the file and change it to another word or phrase.

CHAPTER
13

CUSTOMIZING DOS ON YOUR SYSTEM

Software is the lifeblood of your computer. The hardware may be what you bought, but the software is why you bought it. Whether it's balancing books, designing tapestries, or publishing a monthly newsletter, software applies the computer's power to some task that's important to you; that's why the programs that you use are called *application* programs (programs that handle general computer system housekeeping chores are called *system* programs).

It isn't necessary to learn how to write a computer program to customize DOS so that it better suits the way you use your computer. If you find that you repeatedly use the same series of DOS commands, for example, or consistently use one DOS command with several parameters, you can create your own command that achieves the same result with much less typing.

This chapter shows you how to create your own command files, called *batch files*, and how to use the Doskey command to recycle commands you typed earlier. It also shows you how to modify two special files named AUTOEXEC.BAT and CONFIG.SYS, which contain commands that DOS carries out every time you start or restart your system.

A Batch of Commands

Computers excel at automating repetitious work, so why do we often find ourselves doing repetitious work with our computer? For example, suppose that you frequently use a program, and that before starting the program you use the CD command to make that program's directory the current directory. Instead of typing those two commands each time you run the program, you could put the commands in a file whose extension is BAT (for *batch*, as in a batch of cookies); whenever you typed the name of the batch file, DOS would run both commands just as if you had typed them.

For example, the DOS Editor is a useful program that you may find yourself using quite often. Follow these steps to create a batch file named E.BAT that changes the current directory to DOS and starts the Editor:

1. Change the current directory to DOS by typing `cd \dos`.

2. Start the Editor and tell it to create a file named E.BAT, by typing the following:

    ```
    edit e.bat
    ```

3. When the Editor displays its opening screen, type these two lines:

    ```
    cd \dos
    edit
    ```

4. Choose *Exit* from the File menu to leave the Editor and return to DOS.

5. When the Editor asks whether you want to save the file, choose *Yes.*

Change the current directory to the root by typing `cd \`. Now, to test your first batch file, press E and Enter. DOS should start the Editor; press Esc to clear the screen and choose *Exit* from the File menu to leave the Editor and return to DOS.

A batch file needn't carry out several commands: It can be worthwhile to create a batch file just to run a single complex command. For example, suppose you found that it was useful to use the Dir command to display the files grouped by extension, with the names in alphabetic order within each group; you'd like to limit the display to file names only (no subdirectory names), and, because some directories contain more files than can be displayed in a single screen, you'd like to pause the output after each screenful. The Dir command lets you do all that; type the following to change to the DOS directory and see the result of this Dir command:

```
cd \dos
dir /oen /a-d /p
```

DOS displays the first screenful of files:

```
Volume in drive C is MS-DOS_6
Volume Serial Number is 198C-7A04
Directory of C:\DOS

VFINTD   386      5295 12-06-92   6:00a
E        BAT        15 10-16-93   9:05a
DBLSPACE BIN     65402 12-06-92   6:00a
CHOICE   COM      1754 12-06-92   6:00a
COMMAND  COM     53405 12-06-92   6:00a
DISKCOMP COM     10620 12-06-92   6:00a
DISKCOPY COM     11879 12-06-92   6:00a
DOSKEY   COM      5883 12-06-92   6:00a
DOSSHELL COM      4620 12-06-92   6:00a
EDIT     COM       413 12-06-92   6:00a
FORMAT   COM     22070 12-06-92   6:00a
GRAPHICS COM     19694 12-06-92   6:00a
HELP     COM       413 12-06-92   6:00a
KEYB     COM     14983 12-06-92   6:00a
LOADFIX  COM      1131 12-06-92   6:00a
MODE     COM     23521 12-06-92   6:00a
MORE     COM      2546 12-06-92   6:00a
MOUSE    COM     56408 12-06-92   6:00a
SYS      COM      9364 12-06-92   6:00a
Press any key to continue . . .
```

Near the top of the list is the batch file you just wrote, E.BAT (for *batch*), followed by many files whose extension is COM (for *command*). These COM files contain the programs that make DOS commands work. Press a key to see the next screenful; the extension changes to CPI, (DLL), and then EXE (for *executable*, another type of program file). Continue pressing a key until you reach the end of the list.

The /O (for *order*) parameter in the Dir command is followed by two codes: the E means list the files by their extension, and the following N means that within each group of files with the same extension, order the files by name. The /A (for *attribute*) parameter is followed by a minus sign (which means *not*) and a D (for *directory*), which means don't include file names that refer to directories. As you learned in previous chapters, the /P (for *pause*) parameter tells DOS to display the first screenful of output with *Press any key to continue . . .* in the bottom line, then to wait for you to press a key before displaying the next screenful.

It would be a pain to type that long Dir command every time you wanted to see the files grouped this way, but you don't have to: Just create a batch file named DX.BAT (for *D*irectory by e*X*tension) that contains that Dir command:

1. Type e to start the Editor using your new batch file.

2. Press Esc to clear the screen, then type that Dir command:

   ```
   dir /oen /a-d /p
   ```

3. Exit the Editor; when it prompts you for a file name, type dx.bat.

When you return to the command prompt, try your new batch file by typing dx. You should see the same first screenful of files that you saw a moment ago, except this time there should be two files whose extension is BAT: E.BAT and DX.BAT. If you want to stop the display of file names, press Ctrl+Break to halt the batch file. When DOS asks, *Terminate batch job?*, press Y.

Naming and Storing Batch Files

The names of the two batch files you created give some hint of their purpose. You could make the names longer, if you wanted to make their names more clearly indicate their purpose. Don't, however, give a batch file the same name as a DOS command. When you type something at the command prompt, DOS first checks to see whether you typed one of its built-in commands, such as Dir or Copy. If you didn't, it then checks to see whether you typed the name of a file whose extension is COM or EXE. Failing that, it checks to see whether you typed the name of a file whose extension is BAT. (If it still doesn't find what you typed, it displays the message *Bad command or file name* and shows you the system prompt again.

If you give a BAT file the same name as a built-in DOS command or a file whose extension is COM or EXE, then DOS won't even check to see whether there is a file by that name whose extension is BAT, let alone carry out the commands that it contains. It's as if the file doesn't exist.

You stored the two batch files you created in the DOS directory. This really isn't a good place for your batch files; it's best to reserve the DOS directory just for DOS files, so that when you install a new version of DOS, you—or DOS—can safely delete all the files in this directory without fear of losing any other files. There's a good chance that you'll create a number of batch files as you use your system more. It's a good idea to put them in a directory of their own— one named BATCH—so you'll always know where to look when you want to change one. That doesn't mean that you'll have to change to the Batch directory every time you want to use a batch file, however; it simply means that you'll have to add the Batch directory to your command path.

The DOS Command Path

Whenever you type something at the command prompt, DOS assumes that you typed a command and searches the current directory for the command file (a file whose extension is COM, EXE, or BAT). But what if the command file is in a different directory? You could type the complete path name of the command, but that quickly gets tedious; not only do you have to do all that extra typing, you've got to remember where each file is stored.

But there's a better way. DOS lets you identify one or more directories where it should look for a command file if the command file isn't in the current directory. This collection of directories is called the *command path*. It's easy to check whether a command path is defined for your system; type path.

The Path command with no parameters tells DOS to display the command path currently defined. The response to the Path command should look something like this:

```
PATH=C:\DOS;C:\WINDOWS;C:\BATCH;C:\WORD;C:\TT
```

Your response from DOS will definitely be different. In fact, DOS may respond *No path*, which means that no command path is defined and you can only use programs whose program file is in the current directory. If that's the case, you'll take care of that in a moment.

But if there is a command path, your screen reads *PATH=* followed by a series of directory names separated by semicolons. These *path names* describe the path of directories that DOS must follow, starting with the root, to find a command file that isn't in the current directory. You saw this in the Shell when you started at the root and traced a path down through directories to find a particular subdirectory or file. As you've seen in the last few chapters, the command prompt displays the path from the root to the current directory.

If you create a directory named BATCH, add it to the command path, and store all your batch files there, you can run any batch file no matter what the current directory is. First, type the following to create a directory named BATCH in the root directory and make it the current directory:

```
md \batch
cd \batch
```

DOS doesn't tell you that it created the directory; it just displays the command prompt. The only time you would see a response would be if DOS couldn't create the directory.

Now you'll add Batch to your command path. If DOS responded *No path* to the Path command a moment ago, type the following to define a command path that includes the DOS directory:

```
path=c:\dos
```

As you add more programs and create more directories, you'll find your command path growing longer. DOS imposes two limits that could eventually affect your command path: An individual path name is limited to 64 characters, and the entire Path command is limited to 127 characters.

If DOS responded to the Path command by displaying the directories in your command path, you don't want to type a Path command that names just \DOS and \BATCH, because a Path command replaces any command path in effect; if you typed this short Path command you'd lose any other directories now in your command path. But you can add the Batch directory to your command path without having to retype the entire command path; you'll let DOS do most of the work by creating another batch file.

Letting DOS Create a Batch File

A few moments ago, you typed *path* with no parameter to display the current command path. To define a command path, you type *path* followed by an equal sign and the names of the directories to be included in the command path, separated by semicolons. Look at the response to your Path command again: It starts off *PATH=* followed by the path names of the directories in the command path, separated by semicolons. The response has the same form as a valid Path command.

In an earlier chapter, you redirected the output of the Dir command to a file by including the > character after the command name and before the file name. If you redirected the output of the Path command to a file, the file would contain a Path command that defines the current command path. Do it; you should be in the Batch directory. Type the following to redirect the output of the Path command to a file named SETPATH.BAT:

```
path > setpath.bat
```

Now all you have to do is add \BATCH to the list of directories in the Path command. Type the following to start the Editor and load SETPATH.BAT:

```
edit setpath.bat
```

When the Editor displays the file—it consists of just the Path command—move the cursor to the end of the command and type the following (don't overlook the semicolon at the beginning):

```
;c:\batch
```

Exit the Editor and respond *Yes* when it asks whether to save the file.

Now type the following to change the command path with SETPATH.BAT and display the resulting command path:

```
setpath
```

```
path
```

DOS responds by displaying the command path, which should be just like the one it displayed before, with the addition of *C:\BATCH* at the end. Now you can use the batch files in the Batch directory— you just created the first one—no matter what the current directory.

CONFIG.SYS and AUTOEXEC.BAT

Each time you turn on your computer, or restart it by pressing either the reset button or Ctrl+Alt+Del on the keyboard, the commands contained in two files stored in the root directory are carried out. These files let you tailor how DOS operates, to match the hardware and software installed on your system.

The first of these files to be processed is named CONFIG.SYS (for *configuration* and *system*). It contains special commands called *configuration* commands that tell DOS how to manage the devices attached to your computer and how to manage the memory installed in your computer. Whenever you attach a new device, and frequently when you install a new program, chances are that the setup program for the programmer will change this file (if the programmers were polite, the setup program will ask your permission before changing the file).

To see what's in your CONFIG.SYS file, type the following:

```
cd \
type config.sys
```

You should see some commands like this:

```
      dos = high,umb
   device = c:\dos\himem.sys
   device = c:\dos\emm386.exe noems
devicehigh = c:\dos\ansi.sys
  buffers = 20
    files = 40
   stacks = 9,256
     fcbs = 1
lastdrive = n
    shell = c:\dos\command.com c:\dos\ /e:1000 /p
```

Yours will be different, but several of the commands—particularly the first two or three—should be quite similar.

The second file that is executed when you start your system is called AUTOEXEC.BAT (for *automatic execution*); it contains the same sort of commands that any other batch file might contain. The difference is that DOS carries out the commands in AUTOEXEC .BAT every time the system starts or restarts, before anything else can be done. This lets you tailor the system to your liking: You can have DOS start the Shell automatically, or perhaps start a menu program, or even bring up your favorite word processor or spreadsheet program, if that's how you always begin your sessions.

DOS doesn't require an AUTOEXEC.BAT file, but you almost certainly have one, because DOS creates one while it's being installed. Type the following to see what's in your AUTOEXEC.BAT:

```
type autoexec.bat
```

Again, DOS displays a series of commands something like this:

```
@echo off
path=c:\dos;c:\windows;c:\batch;c:\word;c:\tt
break on
set temp=c:\temp
set comspec=c:\dos\command.com
LH /L:1,56928 c:\dos\mouse.com
LH /L:1,6400 c:\dos\doskey
LH /L:0;1,42480 /S C:\DOS\SMARTDRV.EXE
```

This batch file contains eight commands that are executed each time your system is turned on or restarted. You've seen two of these commands (Prompt and Path) but not the others. As with CONFIG.SYS, when you install new hardware or software the setup program may change—or offer to change—AUTOEXEC.BAT, in order to accomodate the change to your system.

As you learn more about your system, you may want to change these files to better suit your preferences and habits. For example, you created a new directory for batch files earlier in this chapter; if you plan to use this directory, you should use the DOS Editor to edit AUTOEXEC.BAT and add C:\BATCH to the end of the Path command, just as you did when you edited SETPATH.BAT.

Controlling How Your System Starts

Sometimes after you install a program or make some changes to CONFIG.SYS or AUTOEXEC.BAT, your system won't run properly; on rare occasions, it might not even start. If this happens, you can tell DOS to start without carrying out the commands in either CONFIG.SYS or AUTOEXEC.BAT by holding down the Shift key when DOS displays the message Starting MS-DOS . . .. You won't want to use your system after it starts this way—chances are your mouse and some other devices won't work and DOS probably won't have as much memory available as it should—but you can identify the offending command by putting rem (for remark, which tells DOS not to carry out the command) at the beginning of the new or changed commands, one at a time, until the system works properly. Then you can either correct or delete the command that caused the problem.

A somewhat less drastic troubleshooting technique lets you choose which of the commands in CONFIG.SYS to carry out. When DOS displays the message Starting MS-DOS . . . at startup, press and release the F8 key. DOS will ask you whether or not to carry out each command in CONFIG.SYS. This automates the process of isolating the offending command if it's in CONFIG.SYS.

You can also define two or more alternate configurations using different combinations of configuration commands, then choose which one you want to use each time you start DOS. If you sometimes attach to a network, or occasionally use a device that requires a specialized program (called a *device driver*), you could put the commands required to run those programs in a separate configuration and choose that configuration only when you need it, avoiding the need to tie up memory unnecessarily.

Customizing Your Command Prompt

Unless it has been redefined for your system, the command prompt consists of the drive letter of the current disk and the path name of the current directory, ended by a greater-than sign—for example, *C:\DOS>*. This isn't the only possible form of the command prompt; you can define the command prompt to be almost anything you like. Now, switch to the DOS directory by typing:

```
cd \dos
```

You use the Prompt command to define the command prompt; the general form of the Prompt command is:

prompt *text*

The *text* can be anything you'd like the prompt to say. For example, type the following command to make your system polite:

```
prompt May I help you?
```

This command prompt tries to be helpful, but is less informative than its predecessor (it doesn't tell you anything about the current drive or directory):

```
May I help you?_
```

In addition to ordinary text, as in the previous example, the Prompt command recognizes several codes that begin with a dollar sign ($); these codes tell DOS to include specific information or characters in the command prompt. For example, $P means the drive letter and path to the current directory; type the following to define the prompt as the current directory displayed between brackets:

```
prompt [$p]
```

Now the prompt looks more like it used to:

```
[C:\DOS]
```

Here are the the codes you can use in the Prompt command:

$Q	= (Equal sign)
$$	$ (Dollar sign)
$T	Current time
$D	Current date
$P	Current drive and path
$V	MS-DOS version number
$N	Current drive
$G	> (Greater-than sign)
$L	< (Less-than sign)
$B	¦ (Vertical bar, or pipe character)
$H	Backspace (Erases previous character)
$E	Escape character (ASCII code 27)
$_	Start a new line

You can use as many of these codes as you like to define your prompt, plus any text you want. For example, you could define a multi-line prompt (using the $_code to break the lines) that shows the version of DOS, the date, and the current directory:

```
prompt $v$_$d$_$p
```

This prompt takes up quite a bit of room on your screen:

```
MS-DOS Version 6.00
Sat 10-16-93
C:\DOS
```

You'd probably soon tire of a prompt that takes up this much room to tell you things you mostly know already. The current drive and directory is the most useful item of information available to you in the Prompt command. When you find a prompt you like, you can put the Prompt command that defines it into AUTOEXEC.BAT so that DOS will always use your command prompt.

Doskey at Your Service

Another change that would be worth making to your AUTOEXEC .BAT file right now would be to add the Doskey command. Doskey has several features, but the most immediately useful one is its ability to keep track of the commands you enter at the command prompt and let you recycle them. You'll be amazed at the typing you can save by being able to reuse commands you typed earlier.

The Doskey command leaves a small program running in the computer's memory after you enter the command; this program is what lets it keep track of your commands. Doskey may already be loaded; the easiest way to tell is to look at AUTOEXEC.BAT; type the following to load AUTOEXEC.BAT into the Editor:

```
cd \
edit autoexec.bat
```

When the Editor displays the commands in your AUTOEXEC .BAT file, see if one of them mentions Doskey (the command could be *doskey* or *loadhigh doskey*, perhaps followed by some other parameters). If you see such a command, exit the Editor.

If AUTOEXEC.BAT doesn't contain a Doskey command, add one by positioning the cursor at the beginning of the line following the last line and typing:

```
loadhigh doskey
```

Exit the Editor, telling it to save the changed file.

Note

The Loadhigh command tells DOS to load the Doskey program into high memory, an area of memory not normally used by other programs. Doing this leaves more memory available for your application programs. If your computer can't load a program into high memory, DOS simply ignores the Loadhigh command and loads Doskey normally.

Back at the command prompt, there's no more to do if you found a Doskey command in AUTOEXEC.BAT. If you added one, it won't take effect until the next time you start the system, so type one to take effect now:

```
loadhigh doskey
```

It doesn't take long to see the benefits of Doskey. Type the following to change to the DOS directory and list the files whose extension is TXT:

```
cd \dos
dir *.txt
```

The Dir command output shows two TXT files:

```
Volume in drive C is MS-DOS_6
Volume Serial Number is 198C-7A04
Directory of C:\DOS

APPNOTES TXT      9058 12-06-92   6:00a
README   TXT     42618 12-06-92   6:00a
        2 file(s)       51676 bytes
                     16742400 bytes free
```

Now press the up arrow key. The Dir command you typed appears following the command prompt. Press up arrow again, and the CD command you typed before that appears. If you press Enter when either of these commands is displayed, DOS carries out the command just as if you had typed it. More useful yet, you can edit these commands if you need a command close to something you typed before.

Suppose that you wanted to list the files in \DOS whose name starts with D and whose extension is HLP. Press the down arrow key, and the Dir command is back. Press Backspace five times to erase *.TXT, type d*.hlp, and press Enter. DOS lists four HLP files:

```
Volume in drive C is MS-DOS_6
Volume Serial Number is 198C-7A04
Directory of C:\DOS

DEFRAG   HLP      9227 12-06-92   6:00a
DOSSHELL HLP    161323 12-06-92   6:00a
DOSHELP  HLP      5744 12-06-92   6:00a
DBLSPACE HLP     35851 12-06-92   6:00a
        4 file(s)     212145 bytes
                    16740352 bytes free
```

You'll find that a great many of the commands that you type are variations on a few basic forms. Doskey can easily save you one-third or more of the typing you would otherwise do.

When you're editing a command that you have recalled with Doskey, you can move the cursor back and forth with the left and right arrow keys, either insert or overstrike characters (pressing the Ins key alternates between insert and overstrike, just as it does in the Editor), and delete characters by pressing the Del key.

To see all the commands that Doskey remembers, press the F7 key; you'll see a numbered list of commands:

```
1: cd \dos
2: dir *.txt
3: dir d*.hlp
```

You can pick a command from this list by pressing F9; DOS prompts you to enter the number of the command you want to use:

```
Line number:
```

Press 2 and Enter, and the Dir command asking for TXT files is on the command line. You can press Enter to run it as is, edit it and run the revised version, or press Esc to clear it from the command line. Press Esc.

This limited example barely illustrated the power of Doskey. Its advantages multiply rapidly as you type more commands. To see more about Doskey's features, type `help doskey`.

Chapter Review

That's it for this guide to DOS. There's much more to DOS than was covered here, but you've seen the high points of both the Shell and DOS commands. The online help in both the Shell and the command prompt offer a lot of information about the commands not covered here. Now that you have completed this tour, you should be able to go back to the manual and make better use of the information it contains, too. You've come a long way; DOS might still be a challenge, but it should no longer be a mystery.

The most important points covered in this chapter:

- You can put DOS commands in a file whose extension is BAT—a *batch file*—and run all the commands just by typing the name of the batch file.

- It's usually more convenient to store all your batch files in their own directory.

- If you give a batch file the same name as a built-in DOS command or a file whose extension is COM or EXE, DOS will never run the batch file.

- The command path names the directories where DOS should look for a command file if the command file isn't in the current directory.

- If the output of a command is a valid DOS command, you can create a batch file that contains the command automatically by redirecting the output of the command to the batch file.

- CONFIG.SYS is a file that contains configuration commands that are run every time the system is started or restarted.

- AUTOEXEC.BAT is a file that contains DOS commands that DOS runs every time the system is started or restarted.

- To track down problems, you can start DOS without carrying out the commands in either CONFIG.SYS or AUTOEXEC .BAT, or you can choose whether to carry out the commands in CONFIG.SYS one by one.

- You can define more than one set of configuration commands in CONFIG.SYS and choose one set when you start the system.

- You can define your own system prompt with the Prompt command.

- The Doskey command keeps track of the commands you type and lets you reuse them.

INDEX